MW01145462

The Revel
Book 1 of the Foun... ...pon ..ace ..ies

Eddie Snipes

A book by:
Exchanged Life Discipleship

Copyright © 2015 by Eddie Snipes and
Exchanged Life Discipleship

http://www.exchangedlife.com

ISBN: 978-0692414583

Contact the author by visiting http://www.eddiesnipes.com or http://www.exchangedlife.com

Picture Credits
Front cover photo(s) purchased at:
http://www.dreamstime.com

Table of Contents

What is Grace

Before we get into the heart of this book's goal – to grow in grace – it is first necessary to understand what grace is and why it is important. In this modern church era, grace has become one of the most misunderstood teachings of the Bible. People fear what they do not understand. It's not uncommon for misinformed criticism to be leveled against grace by both preachers and church members. Most criticism is based on a lack of understanding of what the Bible is teaching on grace.

On top of the fear of grace teaching there is the problem of under-defining grace. The church tends to water down God's grace to a state where it is only one of the resources we use to help *us* do things for either ourselves or God. I also once thought of grace as a pillar in my theological framework. It was not until I learned that grace is the foundation everything is built upon that I began to understand this amazing Christian life.

Grace strips the flesh of all its glory as it reveals this one basic truth – everything is by God, for God, and to glorify God. Grace invites man into God's fellowship of agape love where we discover that grace is to the benefit of man, glory of God, and nothing is lacking. Grace teaches that we have already been given all things through Christ, God has already satisfied the law's demand for justice, and we are purified so we can stand before God unblemished, uncorrupted, and uncondemned. Until a Christian understands grace, they are torn by a conflicting religious system where God requires faith but the flesh requires self-glory through human performance.

Grace eliminates everything except the glory of God's love for us. Religion says, "You must do more for God." The law says, "You can never do enough to measure up to God." Grace says, "Religion and law have become obsolete. Christ has accomplished all things and God merits us with the work of Christ when we put our trust in Him."

Grace can be summarized in this statement, "Grace is the love of God delivered to us through the person of Christ as a free gift." It cannot be earned or merited. In fact, the moment you try to earn grace it becomes unattainable. Consider the words of **Romans 4:4-5**

> 4 Now to him who works, the wages are not counted as grace but as debt.
>
> 5 But to him who does not work but believes on Him who justifies the ungodly, his faith is accounted for righteousness,

The Bible is explaining that we are in debt to God. We'll explain this in better detail in the following chapters, but this passage is teaching us that if we attempt to earn God's favor, it is impossible. The moment we put God to a merit system, He applies all our works to our debt. Our works of human effort do not earn grace, but are counted toward our debt of sin.

You and I can never put God in debt. There will never be a time when we can do enough good deeds to make God obligated to give us salvation, a blessing, or any rewards. Grace is the expression of God's love to us, but once we try to make God owe us love, God presents our debt to us. Love cannot be earned, and the more we try to do things to make God owe us His favor, we are doing nothing but paying toward a debt that can never be satisfied.

But grace says that when we don't work but believe on Christ, who justified us when we were still in our sins, and it becomes God's pleasure to credit us with His righteousness. The Bible says that without faith it is impossible to please God. But when we trust in God's gift of grace through Christ and believe in His forgiveness and justification, we are accounted righteous as though sin did not exist in us.

The Bible says you are the righteousness of God in Christ. It was never your righteousness that pleased God. It is God's righteousness that pleases God. Scripture also teaches that our best acts of righteousness are filthy rags in God's eyes. A person with a sinful nature can never produce something pleasing to a God with a righteous nature. Sin cannot produce righteousness, nor can righteousness emerge from a nature that is corrupted by sin.

And this is what the grace of God is all about. Mankind tries to glorify himself up to God's level, but God has declared, "No flesh shall glory in My presence." It isn't sin that repels God. It is self-righteousness.

Contrary to what you may have been taught, God does not hate the sinner. Contrary to what you may have heard, God is not pleased with people who try to make themselves righteous. When you look at the life of Jesus, you see this clearly. Jesus' enemies complained that He was a friend of sinners.

Do you realize that Jesus never called a sinner out for their faults? He didn't criticize the thieves, prostitutes, drunkards, and riffraff of society. Most of His twelve disciples were outcasts from the religious community.

Also Consider the woman caught in adultery. Why did the religious leaders bring the adulterous woman to Jesus? They didn't need His approval to execute her. Their goal was to condemn Jesus with the woman. That is the heart of legalism. It produces pride so the legalist is blind to their own sin, but very critical of the sins of others. It also measures the legal standing of others based on what someone does or doesn't do compared to our selfish form of religion. That's why the sin stained legalists felt justified in condemning the sinless Jesus. Jesus was an offender, not because of sin, but because He didn't conform to a human-crafted legalistic standard.

Let me define legalism for the reader. Legalism is any human effort by which we attempt to justify ourselves before God. Legalism is doing something to make the religious person legally equal to God on some level. It is to attempt to make God accept us for the good we do, or to expect credit for the sins we don't do. It's the attitude that God owes us justification for our religion, or owes us a reward for our works.

Legalism believes God legally owes us for human efforts of religion. A legalist points out and condemns the forms of legalism in others while believing their own self-efforts are not legalism. But all religion based on what we do for God is legalism. Anything we do that we think obligates God to accept, forgive, or reward us is legalism. Anything we deprive ourselves of that requires God to reward or accept us is also legalism. In

What is Grace?

other words, any religious practice that is man-dependent has legalism as its foundation.

Legalism hates grace, for grace strips man of his self-glorification. Just as the legalist pointed to the law and demanded Jesus condemn the sinner or be condemned Himself, modern legalism also demands we conform to a standard dependent upon man or be condemned by religious people. Legalism may tolerate a mixture of faith and legalism, but will not tolerate faith in Christ alone. Legalism tolerates sin in the legalist by minimizing it, but quickly condemns sins in others.

Jesus did not confront the adulteress with her sins. She knew she was a sinner. Instead, He confronted her accusers with their sins, for they were just as worthy of judgment and in need of grace just as much as the one they condemned. They stood with stones in hand ready to kill her. Though they presented her to Jesus as a sinner worthy of death, one word of truth from Jesus exposed their condition, causing legalists to become convicted by their own consciences and walked away, leaving their stones behind.

Jesus used the law to condemn those who trusted in the law. They condemned the woman because her guilt was worse than their guilt, or so they thought. To the legalists, Jesus unveiled their condemnation. To the sinner, Jesus unveiled His grace. His final words to her were, "Where are your accusers, is there no one to condemn you? Neither do I condemn you, go and sin no more." Who do you think will have a changed life? The sinner or the legalist trusting in their own efforts to keep the law?

Also consider the woman at the well as told in John 4. This woman was an outcast from the outcasts. Her first strike against her was that she was a Samaritan. A Samaritan was someone whose Jewish parents or grandparents married a non-Jew. They were considered a polluted bloodline and were cut off from the rest of the Jewish society. They were so low in that society that the Jews called people 'Samaritans' as an insult.[1]

---

[1] John 8:48

This woman was considered a lowlife even in the Samaritan community. She was a five-time divorcee who was now shacking up with a man who wasn't her husband. And this is in a culture where a once divorced woman would have been ill thought of, and living as an unmarried partner would cause finger-pointing and gossip. Her reputation was so shameful that she did her work during the heat of the day when the other women would be in their homes.

In the heat of the day, Jesus came to the well to rest. It was an odd place to rest, since the well would not have been a place of shelter. But He came to meet this woman. He did not condemn her for her lifestyle, instead He showed her the way of life and allowed her to be the first person to share God's love with her community.

There was only one group of people Jesus called sinners – those who trusted in their own righteousness. When the rich ruler came to Jesus proclaiming that he had fulfilled the law from his youth up, Jesus dismantled his self-righteousness by giving him the full measure of the law. When the Pharisees claimed to be above those adulterers, Jesus said, "If you have even looked at a woman to lust after her, you have already committed adultery in your heart."

Jesus called the religious leaders broods of vipers, hypocrites, children of the devil, and graves full of death and corruption. He also gave an illustration of grace by showing the pinnacle of moral excellence and the dregs of society. And it wasn't the pinnacle of morality that was justified.

A tax collector went to pray. In that culture, a tax collector (or publican in the King James Version of the Bible) was the worst sinner. They were traitors, for they sold their souls to the Roman Empire to exact taxes from their own people. They were thieves because they could increase their profits by raising taxes to pad their own pockets. They were cruel because anyone who didn't want to pay the extra taxes could be forced to comply by summonsing Roman soldiers to force payment or go to jail. Every Jew hated tax collectors above all else.

Jesus explained that the tax collector prayed, "Lord have mercy on me, a sinner," but the Pharisee thanked God for the fact he had not lowered himself to the tax collectors immoral lifestyle. He thanked God that he fasted several times a week, gave a tenth of his possessions to the poor, and accomplished everything that made him a righteous man.

Jesus said, "The tax collector went home justified by God, but the Pharisee did not." The man trying to please God by what he did was rejected, but the vile sinner who put his trust in God's mercies was justified.

Nothing has changed. God is eager to pour grace into the life of any who trust in Him and not their own works. Consider the words of **Ephesians 1:6**

> To the praise of the glory of His grace, by which He has made us accepted in the Beloved.

The beloved is Christ. You are accepted because of your faith in Christ alone. All God has accomplished to make you perfect serves to fulfill the above passage – that you are justified to the praise of God's grace. You are righteous as God's gift so His grace is glorified. Your life is transformed into a godly character so you can praise the glory of God's grace.

God wants you to see the new life He freely gives and the abundant life Jesus promised and know it is all about His grace – unearned favor toward you. God doesn't want people to glory in their works and say, "I have made myself righteous for you." God wants you to rejoice in God's grace and say, "I stand on this sure foundation because of God's grace. My faults have been removed and I am now righteous because of Your grace."

Grace proclaims that everything good in us only exists because God has gifted us with the goodness that comes only through grace. You are only righteous because righteousness is a gift. You are perfect because God has said, "You are blessed because your lawless deeds were forgiven, your sins were covered, and I will not impute sin to you.[2] I have credited you with My righteousness."[3]

---

[2] Romans 4:7-8
[3] Romans 5:17, Galatians 3:6-9

This is God's plan and no flesh (or works of human effort) will glory in His presence. Yet when this message of God's grace is preached, people blaspheme God's promise by saying that if we live by grace alone, we are in sin. This has been labeled as hyper-grace. I suppose it is, since the Bible declares this truth. Look at **Romans 5:20-21**

> 20 Moreover the law entered that the offense might abound. But where sin abounded, grace abounded much more,
> 21 so that as sin reigned in death, even so grace might reign through righteousness to eternal life through Jesus Christ our Lord.

What reigns? Grace reigns through Christ. But there is another truth that escapes most people because of the translation into English. The New Testament was written primarily in Greek. The passage above says that where sin abound, grace much more abounds. The word 'abound' is the Greek word 'pleonazo', which means to make to increase. It's where we get our word 'plenty' or 'plenteous'.

The word 'much more' abounded is the Greek word 'huperperisseuo', which means to 'super abound' or hyper-abound. It's where our word 'hyperactivity' came from. So yes, hyper-grace is biblical. The concept is that God's grace is NOT an equal and opposite force to sin. God's grace hyper-abounds so sin is overrun and driven out of our lives. So our role is to bind ourselves to the Spirit by faith so grace flows into our life freely and sin is swallowed up by God's victory.

During the era of the apostles, people came into the church after the apostles moved on to start new churches and began teaching people that grace through faith in Christ was good, but not sufficient without man doing his part and keeping the law.

The apostles strongly rebuked this teaching and said the reason these people were corrupting the gospel is because, "They want to bring themselves glory by making a good showing in the flesh."[4]

---

[4] Galatians 6:12-13

What is Grace?

The challenges of the church hasn't changed. People who trust in Christ apart from human effort are still called faithless and accused of not obeying the truth. This is in spite of the Bible's warning from **Galatians 3:1-3**

> [1] O foolish Galatians! Who has bewitched you that you should not obey the truth, before whose eyes Jesus Christ was clearly portrayed among you as crucified?
>
> [2] This only I want to learn from you: Did you receive the Spirit by the works of the law, or by the hearing of faith?
>
> [3] Are you so foolish? Having begun in the Spirit, are you now being made perfect by the flesh?

What disobedient act were they committing that turned them from the truth? They were turning back to the law and losing sight of the fact that their faith began with trusting in Jesus alone. They received the Spirit by the hearing of faith. We also received the Spirit by the hearing of faith – which is the preached and taught word of God.

The Christian life is lived the same way it is entered. We are saved by grace through faith, it is not of works so that no one can boast.[5] Nothing changes. We live by grace through faith. Everything is a gift of God and nothing is by works so none of us can boast. It is all to the praise of His grace.

Grace is God's love given to you through Christ in the form of all things that pertain to life and godliness.[6] Faith is God's invitation for you to enter the gift of grace by trusting in Christ. To fully understand this, it's necessary to spend the next few chapters looking at how our sinful nature came to be, why the law makes sin abound so grace can more abound, and how the cross removed sin so we could receive new life.

---

[5] Ephesians 2:8-9
[6] 2 Peter 1:3

Discussion Questions

Read Titus 2:11-14. Do we work to produce grace or does grace produce a heart for good works?

What does the word 'legalism' mean?

How does legalistic thinking distract a Christian from Christ?

When we try to do something to make God accept us, are we trusting in ourselves or in Christ?

What does Romans 4:4 mean when it says our works are not counted as grace but as debt?

Does it benefit Christians when teachers neglect the Bible's teaching on grace out of a fear that people might sin?

Look again at Titus 2. Does grace create a heart for righteousness or does it invite sin?

Why do people sin while claiming to be under grace?

Why did Jesus often condemn religious people but refused to condemn prostitutes, adulteresses, drunks, and other blatantly sinful people?

Why were sinners drawn to Jesus, but the religious leaders repelled from Him?

Does the church draw sinners today or repel them?

How can we minister as Jesus did?

Review Romans 5:20. If the law causes sin to abound, can we become more righteous by focusing on the law?

Why Do People Need Salvation?

There are two important facts we should understand about our need for salvation. First, you are a sinner. Second, God demonstrated His love for you by bearing all sin in His own body to take it out of the way.

There was once a man who was righteous because He was a partaker of God's righteousness. He didn't make himself righteous and did nothing to earn God's favor. In fact, he never even thought to question his righteousness until a sly creature showed up. This creature persuaded the man and his wife that they could become their own source of righteousness.

"I know how you can be like God," the tempter said. "You can know good and evil. God knows you can have this power, but He doesn't want you to know how to get it."

Of course, this man was Adam and his wife was Eve. What Adam didn't understand is that he already knew good. The only thing missing was sin, or evil. He thought he was about to obtain what God was denying him not knowing that God had already given him all things.

And that is the same deception that plagues mankind today. We still believe God is depriving us, not knowing that God's word not only gives commands that serve as guardrails to keep us out of sin's harm, but also gives us direction for the treasure trove God has abundantly supplied to everyone who believes.

The tactics of the tempter haven't changed. He still convinces people that they can become the source of their own righteousness. He also still convinces people that sin is good to look to and promises to make us wise and satisfied. Both are lies. When a person looks to themselves for righteousness, they can never be satisfied by what they see. We can only deceive ourselves into feeling righteous by comparing ourselves to others whose actions or failures seem worse than our own.

The best temptation can deliver is a moment of gratification, but that's only the mask of sin's empty shell of false promises. Sin is like a drug. The first time we give in it may give us a moment of pleasure, but as the pleasure fades, we are drawn deeper into its labyrinth searching for the promised satisfaction. By the time someone realizes the entrapment of sin, the damage is done. It's much easier to get entangled than it is to escape.

And such was the case with Adam and Eve. The fruit of the tree of the knowledge of good and evil was a call of faith. God said, "I have given you everything but that tree. That tree is the invitation to submit to death, but I have given you the tree of life."

Was God trustworthy? Or was God's goal to deprive man of good? There were no magical properties to the fruit. It was a choice to live by faith or pursue the flesh. It was a call to live by grace through faith, or choose to submit to the law and see if you can make yourself good without God. But that pursuit does not come without sin. We can't be the masters of good without having sin making its claim over us when we fall short.

Most people don't realize it, but the law was introduced to mankind when Adam chose the fruit. God said, "The day you eat of that tree you will surely die." And die Adam did. His physical death was a slow process, but spiritual death was instantaneous. You see, spiritual life cannot exist under the law. The Bible does not call the law a blessing, but a curse. Galatians 3:10 warns, "As many as are of the works of the law are under the curse." The Bible also calls the law the ministry of death. Look at **2 Corinthians 3:5-8**

> Not that we are sufficient of ourselves to think of anything as *being* from ourselves, but our sufficiency *is* from God, who also made us sufficient as ministers of the new covenant, not of the letter but of the Spirit; for the letter kills, but the Spirit gives life. But if the ministry of death, written *and* engraved on stones, was glorious...how will the ministry of the Spirit not be more glorious?

Why Do People Need Salvation?

Most people believe that the law is what justifies them before God. Not so. The Bible calls the law a letter that kills. In fact, the Bible also gives the reason the law was given, and that reason seems to be lost on the church that still believes we merit God's favor by keeping the law. Look at **Romans 3:19-20**

> 19 Now we know that whatever the law says, it says to those who are under the law, that every mouth may be stopped, and all the world may become guilty before God.
> 20 Therefore by the deeds of the law no flesh will be justified in His sight, for by the law *is* the knowledge of sin.

The law serves two main purposes. It serves to proclaim our guilt, but it also serves to drive us to Christ. Look now at **Galatians 3:24-26**

> 24 Therefore the law was our tutor *to bring us* to Christ, that we might be justified by faith.
> 25 But after faith has come, we are no longer under a tutor.
> 26 For you are all sons of God through faith in Christ Jesus.

The law was our tutor that pointed us to Christ, but once we are in Christ, we are no longer under a tutor, that is, we are no longer under the law. (See Romans 6:14 and Galatians 5:18) The law served a purpose, but once that purpose was fulfilled, we are no longer under the tutelage of the law. This passage explains where this book is going, but it also explains one of the purposes of the law. The law reveals to you the knowledge of your sin, shows that you are incapable of becoming righteous, and then it delivers you to Christ where the law has been satisfied and righteousness becomes a free gift.

Just as Adam believed the lie that he could become righteous, God's people were also stuck in that mindset. When God delivered the people out of bondage by defeating Pharaoh, as the people journeyed toward the Promised Land, they declared their ability to become righteous for God. The people said, "We will keep and obey all that you command us to do." In essence they were saying, "Deliver to us the law and we will prove our righteousness to you."

In Deuteronomy God declared, "Cursed is everyone who does not confirm all the words of the law by observing them." This meant that anyone who acted in any way that contradicted the law, they were under the curse of the law. This is both actions that break the law and inaction that does not do the requirements of the law. To this the people said, "Amen." Amen means 'may it be so' or 'I agree fully with what has been said'. Also note that the curse is for any who do not keep ALL the law. Even 99.99% is not good enough.

What the religious community of Moses' day did not understand is that by substituting the gift of righteousness with human effort, they were putting themselves into a system that cannot succeed. They were substituting God's righteousness for their own. They were saying, "We don't need to be made righteous. We can measure up to God by what we do." This does not bring the blessing, but a curse.

Galatians 3:10 points back at this event and says, "For as many as are under the works of the law are under the curse." And this was written to the non-Jewish church that was never under the law, but were being persuaded by legalistic teachers that faith in Christ is not enough, they had to commit to keeping the law. Galatians gives a warning that we face the same problems the Old Testament people faced if we submit under the same system that brought condemnation to all.

If you read the Exodus account, you will see that the people were murmuring and complaining from the beginning. They were faithless and unhappy travelers. When they complained about hunger, God fed them. When they said, "Has God brought us into this desert to die of thirst," God gave them water from a rock. The rock is Christ according to 1 Corinthians 10:4. Not one time did God hold their sins against them – even though they were faithless and far from obedient.

Then something changed. They begged to become partakers of the law and God granted their request. Where the call of faith says that God will become our righteousness, the demand of the law says, "You must be perfect in your own

Why Do People Need Salvation?

righteousness." The wages of sin was death, but the penalty of sin was not applied until the people submitted themselves to become keepers of the law.

The law only asks one question: Are you perfect? If not, then you are guilty. The law never rewards obedience. The law only penalizes failures. If you break the law, you cannot persuade a judge to ignore your crime by pointing to all the good things you have done. Nor does any law enforcement officer pursue law-keepers to reward them for keeping the law. I've never been pulled over and given a check for not speeding. The law penalizes. It does not reward. The same is true for God's law.

When the people believed they could make themselves righteous, God gave the law. It was God's way of saying, "Here is what My perfection looks like. Give it your best shot." But don't forget that there is a penalty to those who are under the law. Not one person was judged by the law before God gave it through Moses. The moment the priesthood received the law, Aaron's two sons were killed for profaning the priesthood.

The moment the law was delivered to the people, three-thousand people died when they broke the law and the curse of the law began. Yet even in the law, God showed mercy by not allowing the curse to destroy them all.

Why did God show favor and supply all the needs of the murmurers and complainers before the law, but then judged them for murmuring and complaining after the law? Let's let the Bible explain. **Romans 5:12-14**

> 12 Therefore, just as through one man sin entered the world, and death through sin, and thus death spread to all men, because all sinned--
> 13 (For until the law sin was in the world, but sin is not imputed when there is no law.
> 14 Nevertheless death reigned from Adam to Moses, even over those who had not sinned according to the likeness of the transgression of Adam

Even though the consequences of sin were in the world and all life was subject to physical death, disease, and oppression, God did not judge the individual for their sins until the people were under the law. Before the law, the people sinned, but their sins were not imputed. Once they entered the law, every sin was imputed.

That is the purpose of the law. The law of God is intended to show you and I that we are not righteous. Nor can we ever become righteous. The law is intended to reveal our utter helplessness to become acceptable to God so we are driven to the one place where the law and its penalties have been removed – the cross of Jesus Christ.

God only wants you to understand that you cannot become a god. You cannot attain to the righteousness of God. And through the cross, God has proved that your incapability to become righteous is not a hindrance to His love for you.

All mankind descended from Adam and all have a flesh nature born into sin. Jesus said, "Whatever is born of the flesh is flesh." The Bible also says that no flesh will have glory in His presence. Isaiah 64:6 tells us that all our righteous acts are filthy in God's sight. Add to this the words of **Romans 8:7-8**

7 Because the carnal mind *is* enmity against God; for it is not subject to the law of God, nor indeed can be.

8 So then, those who are in the flesh cannot please God.

This is the first step in understanding the gospel of grace. When you are in the flesh – which everyone is born into the flesh – you cannot please God. Your best works are merely efforts of the flesh, and those who are in the flesh cannot please God. Righteous acts by human efforts are just as much a work of the flesh as adultery, lying, stealing, or any other sin.

Blatant sin is our flesh declaring that we can satisfy ourselves without God. Human acts of righteousness is our flesh declaring that we can become righteous without God. There is no difference. When I try to become righteous for God, I am making myself a rival of Jesus.

Does this seem strange to you? It is for most people because we have been so conditioned to think like the world that we no longer recognize the grace of God. Consider **2 Corinthians 5:21**

Why Do People Need Salvation?

For He [God] made Him [Jesus] who knew no sin *to be* sin for us, that we might become the righteousness of God in Him.

If God has given you His righteousness through Christ, when you try to make yourself righteous for God you are rejecting the gift of God. It is the same as saying, "I don't need your gift, God. I can do better on my own." Trying to justify ourselves by good works is a rejection of Christ.

This is why the law was necessary. God's people never succeeded in keeping the law. Not one generation made it without judgment. Not one person found hope in anything but God's mercies. The law was necessary to drive us to the realization that we cannot be good enough to obtain God's promises. Only then can we understand that everything is a gift and nothing can be earned.

This is why Jesus was so hard on the religious leaders of His day. Compare how Jesus treated the religious elite to the morally bankrupt. Those the religious community called sinners, Jesus never called sinners. He didn't call one prostitute, drunkard, or any of the moral outcasts sinners. Why? Because they knew they were not righteous and had no problem looking to Him for their forgiveness.

Religious people who could uphold the community moral standards believed they were good without God, but they were blind to the reality that they fell short of the law. They only felt successful because they compared themselves to the moral failures of others instead of to the full demands of the law.

People who try to obtain the promise through the law will always be rejected. The Bible gives a word-picture of this through the example of Moses and Joshua. Moses was the lawgiver. He is a picture of the law, that's why the Bible calls it The Law of Moses. He brought the Ten Commandments given by God down from Mount Sinai.

According to the Bible, Moses only failed once under the law. And by our measure, it was a small mistake. After nearly forty years of hearing the people murmuring, his patience was thin. They were again whining about not having water. God said, "Moses, speak to the rock and water will come forth."

Many years earlier, Moses was commanded to strike the rock, so his mistake wasn't hard to understand. But God said to speak to the rock on this occasion. In his frustration, Moses shouted, "Hear now you rebels! Must we bring water out of this rock for you?" He then swung his staff in anger and struck the rock twice.

For this incident, God denied Moses entry into the Promised Land. His one act of disobedience took him out of the promise while a multitude of sinners went unpunished. Remember, the law only asks one question, "Are you perfect?" If the answer is no, then the reward is denied. All of Moses' works, sacrifice, and obedience was nullified by one act of the flesh.

Moses led the people through the desert and to the edge of the promise. Then God took him to the top of a mountain and said, "Look at the promise. You can see it with your eyes, but you shall not enter there."

And that is exactly what the law accomplishes. It leads people to the promise, but the law can never enter there. Just as the Old Testament law took the people to Jesus but could not enter salvation, the picture of this truth was revealed when Moses took the people to the Promised Land, but had to hand the people over to Joshua so they could enter without him.

Just as Moses died when the promise came, the law was done away with when the promise came. 2 Corinthians 3:7-13 tells us that just as Moses' glory was passing away, the glory of the law passed away when that which is more glorious has come – which is the promise through faith in Christ.

Moses, the law, could not enter the promise but had to pass away so Joshua could take the people into the promise. The same was true for the law and grace. The law released its authority to Christ and we enter the promise by following Jesus.

This picture is clearly seen, for the name Joshua has the exact same meaning in Hebrew as Jesus in the Greek. Both names mean 'Jehovah is Salvation'. Salvation is not from the people, but is the provision of God. All the people had to do in order to receive the promise was trust in Joshua and follow him

Why Do People Need Salvation?

into it. In the same way, all we must do to enter the promise of salvation is trust in Christ and follow Him into it.

Each of us inherited a sin nature through the transgression of Adam. We don't become sinners because we committed a sin. We commit sin because we are sinners by nature. In Christ, we receive a new nature (which we'll discuss in detail later), and the sins that once were held against us and blocked us from entering the promise were rolled away.

The Old Testament account also provides a beautiful word-picture for this New Testament promise. Look at **Joshua 3:14-16**

> ¹⁴ So it was, when the people set out from their camp to cross over the Jordan, with the priests bearing the ark of the covenant before the people,
> ¹⁵ and as those who bore the ark came to the Jordan, and the feet of the priests who bore the ark dipped in the edge of the water (for the Jordan overflows all its banks during the whole time of harvest),
> ¹⁶ that the waters which came down from upstream stood *still, and* rose in a heap very far away at Adam, the city that *is* beside Zaretan.

During the strength of the law, sin abounded but this was no barrier to God. Just as it was when the waters overflowed their banks during the flood season and was no barrier to God. In fact, look at the amazing symbolism here. God not only stopped the flood so the people could pass, but the Bible says that the flood waters were rolled all the way back to Adam.

This is not a coincidence. The word-picture is that God is not merely building a bridge over the barrier of sin, but rolling sin back all the way to the beginning so we can cross into the promise as though sin never existed. Jesus (pictured in the form of Joshua) was declaring His victory over all sin. The sin that came down from Adam has now been reversed. Our promise is that we are acceptable to God as though sin never existed!

This is exactly what is taught in **Romans 5:20**

Moreover the law entered that the offense might abound. But where sin abounded, grace abounded much more.

The law made sin abound so that it overflowed the banks of religion, making it impossible for anyone to enter God's promise of life. Even the best swimmer will be swept away by the raging river of sin. But where sin abounds, Jesus brought in grace that not only made a way, but triumphed so completely over sin that it has been pushed all the way back to Adam. It has been eradicated. So then, any who follow Christ into the promise are blessed as though sin never existed in them with the additional promise that sin will never again be imputed.

Take some time to read Romans 5. Every time Adam's failure is mentioned, Jesus' success is given as a comparison. And the comparison is not two equal forces meeting, but Jesus much more overcame Adam's sin. The message is that Jesus' triumph so much more abounded that sin has been swallowed up by victory.

God's grace hyperactively drove sin back to the beginning and now we are free to enter the promises of God without any barrier or hindrance. Those who follow Christ walk freely through what sin once blocked. Outside of Christ the waters rage, denying passage to all who would attempt to enter.

That is what we are saved from. Sin was inherited through our human nature, but sin has been destroyed in Christ and all God requires is that we trust in His victory and receive His righteousness as a gift.

This is why all people need salvation. Not only is human righteousness corrupted by sin, but the sin also stands as a barrier to God's promise. To those who want to try crossing the raging river of sin, God has given the law so they can give it their best shot. Have you ever seen a river during a severe flood? When the violent waters jettison off rocks? Only a fool would dive in, and if he did, survival is not likely. The best he can hope for is to make it back to the shore from where he started.

This is your sin along with the rage of sin as a whole. It sweeps all people downstream with it. But sin has no power against God. Life is on the other side of the river. Death is on the desert side – where man is born. In Christ God not only gets rid of our sin, but sin as a whole is cut off and driven back so that

Why Do People Need Salvation?

you can now enter God's promise on dry ground without fear or human effort.

The message of grace is that God wants you to inherit the promise, and in Christ it's a peaceful journey. Religion is no more than scooping water out of the river with a bucket. A lifetime of scooping will accomplish nothing. Rest from your labors and trust in Christ. Only He has the power to drive back the waters of sin. It's not about you. It's not about your sin. It's not about your love for God or religious works. The law uses sin to drive us out of human effort so we can find salvation through Christ.

It's all about the glory of God's grace. Everything else is futility and fruitless labor.

Discussion Questions

The Book of Leviticus is where God finished delivering the law to the people. The next book of the Bible is Numbers. Read Exodus 15:24-25 and Exodus 17:3-6. Now read Numbers 11:1. What was God's reaction to the people's complaining?

Why did God respond with grace in Exodus, but with judgment in Numbers?

Did God impute sin before the law?

Read Romans 5:13 and Romans 4:7-8. Does God impute sin to the Christian?

Can a person please God by doing good deeds?

Can we become acceptable to God by not sinning? Can we not sin?

What does it mean, "You are the righteousness of God in Christ?"

Can your sins defeat God's righteousness, which He has declared over you?

What is the purpose of the law?

Why did Jesus call the religious leaders children of the devil, but never called drunkards or prostitutes sinners?

Why did Jesus tell religious people they must do more to fulfill the law, but never told a prostitutes, drunkards, and other sinners to keep the law?

Why didn't Moses' life of service and sacrifice make up for his one failure?

How is Moses dying and handing over his authority to Joshua a picture of the law passing and giving its authority to Christ?

Why do we need to be saved?

Why Do People Need Salvation?

How Sin is Removed

One common question that is posed against Christianity is, "Why doesn't God just get rid of sin and take us all to heaven?"

As we have already seen, God has indeed removed all sin and invited us into heaven. If this is true, the question needs to be reworded as, "Why doesn't God just let us live for the flesh and then treat us as though we are like Him?"

Let's put this into perspective. Has anyone ever done something that gets on your nerves? Have you been around someone whose actions are frustrating, but they don't care? What is your reaction? Do you invite them to live with you and make it your responsibility to conform to their habits? Do you hang around people that do things you can't stand?

When someone comes into your house, do you change the house rules and expectations to fit the lifestyles of those you disagree with? No. If you are going to be welcomed into my house, you have to respect our standards. I don't let smokers come into my house and fill it with the stale odor of cigarettes. If they want to smoke, that's their choice, but not in my home. No drugs in my home. No stolen goods, prostitution, tracking mud, or anything else that is not acceptable to the peace of our home.

So now we are going to demand that God go against His own character and nature to conform heaven to our ways? If it doesn't work that way in our lives, why do we demand God passively allow mankind to track mud into His courts? Instead, God graciously cleans off our mud and then welcomes us in.

One thing we as Christians must understand is that we can't make someone want a better lifestyle. When in the army, I had a fellow soldier whose life was in shambles. He was miserable. Three times he attempted suicide. After getting out of the hospital, our commander began the work of discharging him as being incompatible with army life.

The army wasn't his problem. He was depressed and hopeless. He would often sit alone in the dayroom drinking his sorrows away. One day I had the opportunity to sit with him and share the gospel. This was after he complained about how meaningless his life was. After sharing with him for a while he said, "You're wasting your time. I've heard all this before." He quoted a few scriptures to me to prove he knew the gospel. "I'm just not interested in Christianity."

We cannot make someone choose the gospel. There are people who believe sin and all its consequences are better than what God can offer. There are people who believe a life of sorrow and depression is better than what God can offer.

You cannot make someone choose life. You can only unveil life as you pray for the Spirit to reveal Himself to them, but if someone despises the abundant life, beating them with scriptures will not change that. Scaring them with judgment will not change that. It's the goodness of God that leads us to repentance.[7] The unveiling of sin only serves to show the meaningless of our religious efforts and self-righteousness. But seeing our sins does not produce repentance. It drives out the delusion that we can save ourselves so we have the understanding to look to Christ.

Taking sin to heaven would not make us happy. God deciding something is no longer a sin will not make us happy. Something is a sin because it is harmful to us or our relationship with God, or both.

God is our creator. He knows what works, doesn't work, what builds us up, and what tears us down. He knows that we were created to be united with Him, and that anything that draws us away from the purpose for which we were created will leave us empty. God's commands serve to do two things in the Christian's life. They warn us to stay away from what harms us, and it leads us toward the ways that grow us into a mature spiritual person – which is the only thing that can satisfy.

The devil is a scam artist that makes the things that are empty look good so we are deceived into letting him steal what actually has value. A counterfeit bill looks good to the untrained

---

[7] Romans 2:4

How Sin is Removed

eye, but is nothing but a worthless piece of paper to those who know what the real thing looks like.

If you've watched the Antique Roadshow, you have probably witnessed this in action. People come in with rare pieces that they have sometimes paid thousands of dollars for, only to discover it was a worthless forgery. To their untrained eye, it looked valuable, but it was nothing more than a scam to rob them of their money. Temptation is the same way. It is a scam to rob you of God's best by promising you that the flesh has more to offer.

God doesn't accept the corruption of the flesh into His kingdom. Instead, He offers to take us out of the flesh and invites us to walk in the purity of the Spirit. Then every treasure that has eternal value is freely given to us.

God only fills empty hands. Someone holding on to trash cannot receive God's treasure. A friend brought back pictures from the mission field. In this third-world country, families had shanties erected on the edge of a landfill. Daily, they picked through the trash looking for things of value. What they thought was treasure was refuse from someone else's garbage. It only looked valuable because the trash is all they have ever known. But take that person and give them a wealthy home, train them in this new lifestyle, and then take them back to the trash and what happens? They would reject the very things they once treasured.

This is a simple word-picture of the new Christian life, but even it falls far short of what God is doing. God is not only taken us out of the trash, but He also changes our nature.

Before Christ, our old nature sinned because it was in its nature to do so. Why does the unredeemed person hate church and hate hearing the word preached? It's because what they are hearing is contrary to their nature. They may try to do religious things, but it can't last. The more we force ourselves to do what is contrary to our nature, the more miserable we become, and this gives birth to hypocrisy, heresy, or abandoning the faith.

That's why the world looks at the church and thinks we are depriving ourselves of enjoyment. I once had someone tell me that in order to be a Christian, you have to hang your head low and carry a Bible everywhere we go. Yet when you meet someone who is walking with God, their head isn't low. They are abounding with joy. A joy that can never be found in the activities of the world.

To the lost soul, the Christian life is drudgery, for the fleshly nature cannot even comprehend the things of the Spirit. Or as the Bible states in **Romans 8:7**

> Because the carnal mind *is* enmity against God; for it is
> not subject to the law of God, nor indeed can be.

The carnal (or fleshly) mind can't even force itself to be subject to the law of God. And if it tries, it will produce frustration instead of peace. The sinful nature can only understand a sinful lifestyle. It doesn't recognize the lifestyle as sin because it is at home in that way of thinking. The flesh's religion can only produce self-glorification and pride. When these two things are not being accomplished, their faith will be exposed as counterfeit and frustration will build until rebellion against religion emerges. Or they regain control enough to return to self-exaltation.

Everything changes when the Christian is transformed. God doesn't convert us to Christianity. God adopts us into His family and gives us a new nature. When we are born again in the Spirit, our desires change because our nature has changed.

Just as the fleshly nature cannot be comfortable in righteousness, the new nature of the Spirit cannot be comfortable in sin. We can still commit sin, but we cannot find peace there. Satisfaction is impossible, and even when we find pleasure in sin, there is a discomfort in our spirit because we are acting in a way that is contrary to our nature.

When someone first becomes a Christian, many of the fleshly ways of thinking are still part of their habitual life. Because the ways of the flesh create an internal conflict, Christians have one of two responses. The first and best response is to start purging out the old ways as they learn to walk in the Spirit. Unfortunately, the church doesn't teach how to walk in the Spirit, so most of us flounder until we stumble across the right way. But because the wrong way repels from

How Sin is Removed

our spirit, most Christians keep trying to find a way out of sin or fleshly ways of thinking, even though they can't find victory.

The second response is that when a new Christian begins to feel emptiness in sin, they begin trying to find the pleasures they once experienced when they had a sinful nature. When sin fails to gratify, they delve deeper into sin and experiment in the flesh as they desperately seek to find rest for their souls.

Eventually, that Christian will come back and will have a clearer way of thinking. The wayward Christian that returns often becomes a very effective disciple. When attending an evangelism class, each person had to give a testimony. Out of eighteen people, only one of them had the testimony that they began growing without a time of falling away. Most fell back into sin and did many unchristian-like things. But when they realized they had hit spiritual rock bottom, they began looking for answers in the Bible. Because they now understood that the world had no answers, they began learning how to not look to the flesh for hope and fulfillment.

When we recognize this conflict, we are able to better understand our struggles and the struggles of other Christians. It takes away the judgmental spirit because we can identify with their struggles.

Because the unredeemed person only has a self-centered sinful nature, they cannot become spiritual or do spiritual things that do not puff up the flesh. Everything has to be to the gratification of the flesh or it creates internal conflict. The flesh will use anything at its means to feed its ego. This includes politics, charity, random acts of kindness, ministry, church activities, or lust, greed, hatred, and other blatant sins. For the fleshly mind, everything is sin, for everything is the exaltation of the flesh.

The unbeliever will do by nature the things that are rooted in sinful flesh, and the believer will do by nature the things that are rooted in God's righteousness. If we act contrary to our nature, there will always be conflict – both internal and external. Here is a good example found in the Bible. Look at **Romans 2:14-15**

How Sin is Removed

¹⁴ for when Gentiles, who do not have the law, by nature
do the things in the law, these, although not having the
law, are a law to themselves,
¹⁵ who show the work of the law written in their hearts,
their conscience also bearing witness, and between
themselves *their* thoughts accusing or else excusing *them*)

A gentile is anyone that is not a Jew. The Jews were raised under the law, taught the law, and put forth their best effort to keep the law. The Jewish people during the early church times had an entire culture that was built around the law. This included political, economic, religious, and social. From birth every Jew in that era was taught the law.

The gentiles had no exposure to the law. Gentile Christians often came out of pagan cultures that either had many gods or were anti-God. They didn't know the law, were never taught how to keep it, and most had never heard of it. Yet as they came to faith in Christ, something within them changed. Without knowing the law, something within them caused them to act in ways that was in agreement with the law. Suddenly, it was in their nature to act in ways that pleased God.

They were not trying to keep a list of rules. Nor were they making up their own laws. There was nothing external guiding them, yet they were living a lifestyle that those raised under the law could not accomplish. Those raised under the law were trying to live contrary to human nature, and failing, but those without the law were conforming to a lifestyle that defied natural explanation.

The law was written in their hearts, and these people were following the desire of their hearts based on the new nature God had given them. This is not a call to live according to a new Gentile law. It's our example that if we walk by faith, the law takes care of itself. Let me bring in another passage that disarms the argument that the Christian must submit to the law. Look at **Acts 13:38-39**

³⁸ "Therefore let it be known to you, brethren, that
through this Man is preached to you the forgiveness of
sins;

How Sin is Removed

[39] "and by Him everyone who believes is justified from all things from which you could not be justified by the law of Moses.

When trying to explain the gospel to the Jewish people, the apostles made it clear that faith justifies us, and this could not happen under the law. In **Acts 15:9**, the Apostle Peter was answering those who were claiming he broke the law by going into the house of a Gentile and dining with them. This was against the Jewish law, for Gentiles ate and acted in ways that were called unclean in the Old Testament law.

God sent Peter to a gentile's house to preach the gospel of Christ, and when he did so, the Holy Spirit was poured out upon them. Then Peter said, "God made no distinction between us and them, purifying their hearts by faith." The Gentiles didn't do anything according to the law, nor did God call them into the law. There was no difference in God's eyes between the law-keeping Jew who responded by faith, and the lawless Gentile, who responded by faith. Their lives were changed, but not through the law – the Old Testament law that the Bible says could never justify the worshipper.

If we are walking according to our nature, we will do by nature the things that please God. And it will please us, for we and God are sharing the same nature. We'll explain this in detail shortly. First let's look at the work of Christ as it pertains to our new nature.

Out with the Old, In with the New

If someone tries to fix up their old life, they will have limited success at best. Usually frustration and failure is the end result, yet even if we succeed, it's meaningless. God's purpose is not to patch up the old you, but to crucify it. The crucified life is something we'll study in a later book in this series, but the death of our sinful nature is also one of the basics of discipleship. That's why the Apostle Paul said in **Galatians 2:20-21**

[20] "I have been crucified with Christ; it is no longer I who live, but Christ lives in me; and the *life* which I now live in

the flesh I live by faith in the Son of God, who loved me and gave Himself for me.

21 "I do not set aside the grace of God; for if righteousness *comes* through the law, then Christ died in vain."

In other words, if he could have fixed up his old life by keeping the commandments of the law, then it would have been unnecessary for Jesus to have died for him. The Bible also teaches that the weakness of the law is our flesh. Because we had a nature that is not part of God's life, our human spirit is incapable of upholding the law. We were the weakest link, and when we failed, any religious system dependent upon us failed with it. As a new creation, we live by faith in Christ – not by works or human effort.

When Jesus died on the cross, He did not *only* pay the penalty of sin. He nailed our sins to His cross, He nailed the law that condemned us to the cross, and He nailed our old nature to the cross.

When we trust in Christ, God – who is not bound by time – accounts us as righteous because of our trust in Him, puts our sins into the grave, and takes our old nature away and buries it with Christ. The Bible explains this through the ordinance of circumcision.

God gave Abraham the ordinance of circumcision four hundred years before the law was delivered. Circumcision was associated with the Old Testament law, but circumcision was actually the step into God's covenant of promise. Abraham was not under the law, but he was under circumcision.

Circumcision is when the foreskin of a male child is cut away. The child is a newborn, incapable of doing anything or understanding anything. The command to circumcise a child on the eighth day after birth is also symbolic of the Christian life. The cutting away of the flesh was done independently of the child's knowledge, works, or understanding. The child had no knowledge of what was being done and did not participate in the ordinance. He just lay there, incapable of helping in any way, while the priest performed the work.

The covenant with Abraham was the work of God. God asked Abraham to prepare the covenant but did not allow Abraham to participate in swearing the oath. The Bible says that Abraham was put into a deep sleep and was only allowed to witness it in a vision, but the covenant God made with Abraham was an oath between God and Christ – even though it was in the Old Testament. The Bible goes on to explain that the law that came afterward had no bearing on God's covenant with Abraham.[8]

The reason is because God swore the oath with Himself so that it could not be broken by man's failure. Man's only role was to submit to circumcision. The physical act of circumcision in the Old Testament was a foreshadow of the coming New Covenant circumcision of Christ.

In the New Testament, man again prepared the sacrifice by nailing Jesus to the cross, but the oath of God's covenant to us was not between us and God. It was confirmed between God and Christ. God has made His covenant of promise a certainty by eliminating the weakness of man and confirming the promise by Himself alone.

Again, our only role is to submit to God's circumcision. Look at **Colossians 2:9-12**

[9] For in Him dwells all the fullness of the Godhead bodily;
[10] and you are complete in Him, who is the head of all principality and power.
[11] In Him you were also circumcised with the circumcision made without hands, by putting off the body of the sins of the flesh, by the circumcision of Christ,
[12] buried with Him in baptism, in which you also were raised with *Him* through faith in the working of God, who raised Him from the dead.

In Christ was the fullness of God, and through Him you are complete. What needs to be done to complete what has been completed by God?

---

[8] Galatians 3:17

If an artist finished his masterpiece and was satisfied with his work, would he be pleased if you came up and said, "I can make this better," and proceeded to paint your own ideas onto his canvas? No, it would nullify the masterpiece and you would be called a vandal. How much more true is this for God's work. When the Lord looks at His work and declares, "It is finished," and then declares, "You are complete in Christ," but you come up and say, "That's good but I have to do my part," will God be pleased? Certainly not. In fact, you will have vandalized the work of Christ.

Believe God's declaration. You are complete in Christ. Anything you add to it is taking God's perfect work and trying to reestablish it on your flawed human efforts. It is to take the new covenant and try to place it into the law – the place where the weakness of man destroyed the law of God.

Your role is to believe on Christ and let the Spirit do its work in you. The Spirit of God circumcises your old fleshly nature out of you and gives you new life as you are born again into the Spirit. It is a work without hands. In other words, it's God's masterpiece without the interference of human effort.

That is what circumcision symbolizes. Just as the flesh of the male child was cut away so the child could enter into God's covenant of promise, the one who trusts in Christ has their fleshly nature cut away so they can enter into the promise. Or as **1 Corinthians 15:50** puts it,

> Now this I say, brethren, that flesh and blood cannot
> inherit the kingdom of God; nor does corruption inherit
> incorruption.

You cannot enter God's promise or His kingdom in the flesh. The flesh is cut away by the Spirit and buried with Christ. The ordinance of baptism is the testimony of the work of God. Baptism is you being buried to your old life by dying to the flesh and being covered by the water, and raising up into new life by emerging from the grave as a new creation.

Jesus alluded to this when He said, "Unless a grain of wheat falls into the ground and dies, it remains alone. But if it dies, it

　　　　　　　　　　　How Sin is Removed

produces much grain. He who loves his life in this world will lose it, but he who hates his life in this world will find eternal life."

The one who allows God to crucify his old life through faith in Christ will be raised to new life by the power of God. Then you have a new spirit with a new nature where old things have passed away and all things are new and of God.[9]

God foretold of this gift in the Old Testament. Look at this New Covenant promise from the Old Testament as explained in **Ezekiel 36:26-27**

[26] "I will give you a new heart and put a new spirit within you; I will take the heart of stone out of your flesh and give you a heart of flesh.

[27] "I will put My Spirit within you and cause you to walk in My statutes, and you will keep My judgments and do *them.*

Isn't this exactly what we read in the New Testament when those who were born again without even knowing the law, did by nature the things written in the law, proving God had written His law on their hearts? The Christian does not have to keep the law. It becomes our desire to do the things God has written on our hearts. Walking in righteousness is a delight, not a requirement of human effort.

There is a danger every Christian faces. Many would say it is sin, but in reality the greatest danger is the law. Look at **2 Corinthians 3:14-16**

[14] But their minds were blinded. For until this day the same veil remains unlifted in the reading of the Old Testament, because the *veil* is taken away in Christ.

[15] But even to this day, when Moses is read, a veil lies on their heart.

[16] Nevertheless when one turns to the Lord, the veil is taken away.

We've already read passages where those who turn to the law are under the curse. Now we are warned that when our trust

---

[9] 2 Corinthians 5:17-18

is shifted from Christ to the law, a veil covers our eyes and hearts. That veil is only taken away when we turn back to Christ to trust in His works.

We can see this in the Gentile church. When they were walking by faith, they were doing by nature the things written in the law, but their focus wasn't on the law, but Christ. When legalists came in and taught the law to the Gentile churches, we see sin beginning to emerge. The books of Galatians and 1 and 2 Corinthians are great examples. When Jewish Christians who were stuck in the mindset of the law began to teach the Gentiles that they should obey the law, they stopped acting according to their new nature and began trying to obey the law by human effort.

The result was sin, spiritual immaturity, and the Bible says, "You have fallen from grace." It was not a fatalistic proclamation that they were now lost. It was the warning that they could not live out the Christian life by human effort. The works of the law was only a veil that blinded them to the transforming power of the Spirit. Look at the words of **Galatians 5:4-5**

4 You have become estranged from Christ, you who *attempt to* be justified by law; you have fallen from grace.
5 For we through the Spirit eagerly wait for the hope of righteousness by faith.

Two chapters earlier this church was asked, "Who bewitched you that you should no longer obey the truth?" What were they doing that was disobedient to the truth? They were trusting in the works of the law and had forgotten that the Christian life was entered and lived by faith in Christ alone.

Many well-meaning but ill-informed teachers will teach that you are pleasing to God when you keep the rules, but the only rule that matters is the law of faith.[10] The law of faith is to trust in Christ's works and the promise that our transformation is the work of the Spirit in our lives and not the work of ourselves through human effort.

---

[10] Romans 3:27-28

How Sin is Removed

Most Christians don't believe that the Spirit has the power to transform our lives. Many believe they have to help God along by turning back to the law or teaching others to live by law. If someone doesn't believe God can change you, they will erect barriers with rules to protect the Christian from sin. The greater sin is to create our own righteousness. Self-righteousness is never acceptable to God.

Self-righteousness is not only those who look down their holy snouts at the less spiritual. Self-righteousness is also the one who tries to make God accept them by what they do or don't do. The self-righteous is the one who trusts in themselves instead of believing that righteousness is God's gift to us. This is even more subtle when people claim that God's grace empowers us to keep the law. The fact is that you are either focused on Christ or focused on yourself.

The more you look to self to obey God, the more you fall into disobedience. God will never empower you to do what Jesus has already done. God will never help you to accomplish what Christ has already accomplished and fulfilled for you. And yes, the law is fulfilled. **Romans 8:4**

> That the righteous requirement of the law might be fulfilled in us who do not walk according to the flesh but according to the Spirit.

How have we fulfilled the law? It is already done. Jesus fulfilled the law, and by faith in Christ, we are walking in the Spirit where the righteous requirements of the law are fulfilled in us. It is a gift of God's grace that in turn produces the fruit of the Spirit through us. Let's bring in a few other passages to explain this. Let us first revisit Colossians. We have already seen that our sin was taken away – along with the law that accused us. We also looked at the veil of the law that can only be taken away when we look to Christ. Not only does the bondage of the law disappear, but the very thing we hoped to accomplish for God becomes God's gift to us. Look at the rest of that passage in **2 Corinthians 3:17-18**

> [17] Now the Lord is the Spirit; and where the Spirit of the Lord *is*, there *is* liberty.

18 But we all, with unveiled face, beholding as in a mirror the glory of the Lord, are being transformed into the same image from glory to glory, just as by the Spirit of the Lord.

How are we transformed? By what we do? By what we keep ourselves from doing? No. We behold the glory of Christ and the Spirit transforms us into His image. It is the power of Christ's glory being imparted to us through the Spirit of His glory within us. Instead of our glory in self-righteousness, we receive from the only one who truly has glory. And God glorifies Himself through us by changing us.

Our outward behavior will begin to change as the glory of Christ becomes our focus. Do you see that this is not a passage or two taken out of context? This is the consistent theme of the New Testament. Everywhere we look we see the same message. You aren't changed by what you do. Your behavior changes as the Holy Spirit transforms you into the image of Christ. When your eyes are on Christ, you are walking according to your new nature. When your eyes are on the law, you will walk according to the flesh. Study Romans 8. Take special note of verses 4-5. What is of the flesh? The law. What is of the Spirit? Faith in Christ.

Let's end this chapter by bringing in one more passage. This passage sums up what we have been studying by revealing the power of grace to transform our lives. Look at **Titus 2:11-15**

11 For the grace of God that brings salvation has appeared to all men,
12 teaching us that, denying ungodliness and worldly lusts, we should live soberly, righteously, and godly in the present age,
13 looking for the blessed hope and glorious appearing of our great God and Savior Jesus Christ,
14 who gave Himself for us, that He might redeem us from every lawless deed and purify for Himself *His* own special people, zealous for good works.
15 Speak these things, exhort, and rebuke with all authority. Let no one despise you.

How Sin is Removed

Let me ask you a simple question. What is our role in God's work in this passage? It is only to look at Christ. Jesus is full of grace and truth. Jesus was the grace of God that brought salvation to all men, but the work of grace doesn't stop at salvation.

Grace teaches us to deny ungodliness and worldly lusts. Grace teaches us to live soberly, righteously, and godly – even though we are in an age that teaches the opposite. Grace teaches us to look for our hope in Christ alone. What's more, grace creates a purified people who are zealous for good works.

What the law could not do in that it was weak through the flesh, God did by sending His own Son. We now look to Christ and as we trust in Him, the Spirit produces the work of faith in us. Just as righteousness is the gift of God to those who believe, the fruit of the Spirit is God's gift to any who believe.

Those who don't believe that God's grace has the power to do this will never receive. Grace will remain a mystery. It's a mystery because the veil of the law prevents them from seeing what is a free gift through Christ.

Our last word of exhortation in this passage is, "Let no man despise you." This means that when people ridicule your hope in grace, you do not allow them to use peer pressure to drive you back into religion. Just as grace was despised in the early church and the legalists persecuted the Apostle Paul, the same will be true for any who fully trust in Christ.

Very few are opposed to trusting in Christ for part of the work, but as the Bible says, they persecuted those who would not keep the law because they wanted to glory in the flesh.[11] The same is true today. Everyone wants to say, "I have done my part." They want to have part of the glory and feel that God owes them for their service.

The message of grace says that everything is a gift received by faith and nothing is the work of man. Our only role is to trust in the completed work of Christ. We rightly divide the word of truth so we can learn how to walk by faith. We grow into

---

[11] Galatians 6:13

spiritual maturity by learning to receive what Christ has done. Those who trust in grace will receive what can never be accomplished through the law or a mixture of law and grace.

A mixture is polluted. It is a lukewarm faith where we've taken the stone cold law and tried to mix it with the fire of the Spirit of faith. God has said, "I will spew the lukewarm Christian out of my mouth."[12] You cannot mix the law and grace. It's either to the glory of God's grace, or man using religion to steal glory for himself.

A thief of glory receives shame and failure. Yet the one who glorifies God is invited into God's glory. Or as the Bible says, "The one who exalts himself will be humbled. The one who humbles himself will be exalted."[13] You cannot lift yourself up. It's either the work of God, or it is the work of the flesh.

God has removed sin, given you a new nature, made you complete in Christ, and given you all things through Christ. Everything is a gift of God's grace or the perishing efforts of man. Thanks be to God that you and I have this unspeakable gift, and all that is required is that you trust in His grace!

---

[12] Revelation 3:16
[13] Matthew 23:12

How Sin is Removed

Discussion Questions

How would you answer the question, Why doesn't God just get rid of sin and take everyone to heaven?

What happens to the unredeemed person when their religious life fails to give them glory or due recognition?

What motivates the Christian to walk in godliness?

Can a Christian fall into the same way of thinking as the unredeemed?

Why does an unredeemed person do religious things?

What causes hypocrisy? And does hypocrisy discredit the Bible?

Why did the early Gentile Christians live in agreement with the law without trying to keep the law?

Why did God implement circumcision in the Old Testament? How does this help us to understand the New Covenant of Christ?

How is the law fulfilled?

Read 1 Corinthians 2:14-16. If a Christian doesn't trust in the power of the Spirit, will the way of grace appear foolish to the Christian?

Will the Christian who views grace through the flesh think taking away the rules of the law will cause people to sin?

Do Christian rules work to produce spiritual maturity? Why or why not?

Read Titus 2:11-15. What does grace accomplish in us?

Why are Christians tempted to mix law and grace?

Read Romans 11:6, Romans 4:14, and Galatians 3:18. Why can't we mix the law and grace?

Complete Redemption

There is a difference between redemption and forgiveness. Both principles help us to understand the gospel. Forgiveness is God's pardon for our sins. Redemption is when our bondage to debt has been paid by another person. Let's begin by looking at the law of redemption.

In Leviticus 25:47 the Bible begins explaining the law of redemption as it pertains to a person's life. It also explains why slavery is taught in the Bible. Those who haven't studied this topic mistakenly compare the Bible's teachings to the type of slavery we see in the 1700s and 1800s in the US and Europe. People falsely claim that the Bible endorses slavery. The Bible calls that practice 'manstealers' or 'kidnappers'. Forced slavery is strongly condemned in the Bible.

In Leviticus, the Bible explains slavery as a payment for debt. If a man borrows money, he agrees to pay it back by a set date. If he is unable to do so, he must repay with his service as a slave. This is why in the book of Philemon, the Apostle Paul sends the runaway slave Onesimus, back to his master with a letter asking for leniency.

In that era, there was no such thing as wiping out your debt with bankruptcy. If the sum of money being borrowed was large enough, a man could include his entire family as collateral.

In Leviticus, the Bible says that if someone becomes poor and sells himself into slavery, a kinsman who has the means can redeem his relative by paying off the debt. This is a picture of what would one day come through the cross. Every offense against the law in deed, thought, failing to obey, or actively disobeying puts us in debt. Any works we do while we are a slave to sin does not earn any reward or merit. It only goes toward our debt.

This sheds light on Romans 4:4, which we studied earlier. To him who works, his wages are not counted as grace but as debt. A slave never received wages for his work. Whether he put forth the minimum effort or extra effort, his wages did not change. Each day was a service for his debt, and any work performed was for his master and not for himself or his benefit. If an enslaved person did not perform their duty, there was a punishment for failing to serve as agreed upon when they borrowed the money, but there is no extra payment for going the extra mile. Understanding these things helps us to understand the words of Jesus in **Luke 17:7-10**

> 7 "And which of you, having a servant plowing or tending sheep, will say to him when he has come in from the field, `Come at once and sit down to eat '?
>
> 8 "But will he not rather say to him, `Prepare something for my supper, and gird yourself and serve me till I have eaten and drunk, and afterward you will eat and drink '?
>
> 9 "Does he thank that servant because he did the things that were commanded him? I think not.
>
> 10 "So likewise you, when you have done all those things which you are commanded, say, `We are unprofitable servants. We have done what was our duty to do.'"

Many translations interchange the word 'servant' and 'slave'. Both come from the Greek word 'doulos' which means servant, slave, or bondman. It is someone in bondage without the right to be free. This is not a paid servant.

Jesus is explaining that when you labor for righteousness, it profits nothing. It is your duty because you are in debt. No amount of labor can change a slave's condition. A slave cannot labor for his own benefit. He can only do service to his master. Or as the Apostle Paul stated in **Romans 7:14**

> For we know that the law is spiritual, but I am carnal, sold under sin.

Jesus said, "Whoever sins is a slave to sin."[14] Jesus goes on to explain that a slave has no inheritance and will not remain in his master's house forever. That role is only to sons – those who will inherit the kingdom. He then says, "If the Son makes you free, you are free indeed."

---

[14] John 8:34-36

Complete Redemption

All these things work together to paint an amazing picture of grace. Because you sinned, you are now a slave to sin. You owe a debt that you cannot repay because you are carnal (or fleshly). The flesh is incapable of departing from slavery; therefore, something must be done to redeem us out of the flesh's bondage to sin.

This is why Jesus is called our Redeemer. Forgiveness is NOT enough. The debt must be paid. We are debtors to the law and have been sold to sin. A sinner cannot make himself an unsinner. A slave can't work his way out of slavery. Only by paying to price of the debt can a slave ever be made free. Since we are incapable of paying our debt, Jesus became our redeemer, paid the debt with His own blood, and then we have the promise that when Jesus makes us free, we are free indeed.

We are not partially free. Not mostly free. Not free until we sin again. We are free indeed. We'll shortly examine why sin does not make us debtors again, but first we need to understand that our debt is paid because Jesus, who had the means of paying our debt, redeemed us out of the law and set us free from sin.

Let me again reiterate that the word 'redeem' means to have your debt paid in full by another person. When Jesus died on the cross, He cried out, "Tetelestai," which means, "The debt has been paid." This is the Greek word that merchants stamped onto receipts when all payment had been received. Most English Bibles translate this into, "It is finished," but knowing what was finished is of vital importance. It was your debt that was finished, or paid in full.

On the cross, the complete work of God for you was delivered by Jesus. Your sins were forgiven and your debts were paid. He didn't only pay your debts at that moment, but all debt to sin. Keep in mind that all your sins were in the future when Jesus paid the debt. It was not your individual sins that were defeated. It was sin as a whole.

When you sin, Jesus doesn't reapply the blood to cover it again. I grew up hearing that when we sin, we ask God for forgiveness and then God reapplies the blood to cover our sins each time we confess.

Complete Redemption

This simply is not true and the Bible expressly refutes this idea. In fact, the concept that we must keep confessing and asking for forgiveness again and again is disbelief in what God has said. The normal human logic is to question God and say something like, "This means we'll get away with sin." Of course it does! That is the entire message of redemption. We are not paying for our sins. We are trusting in Jesus who paid the debt for all sin.

In another chapter we'll answer the question, what about sin? But that's a separate topic and has nothing to do with Jesus' forgiveness and redemption. The Bible says that sin cannot be paid twice. Jesus doesn't suffer each time we sin. This very topic was addressed in **Hebrews 9:25-26**

> 25 not that He should offer Himself often, as the high priest enters the Most Holy Place every year with blood of another--
> 26 He then would have had to suffer often since the foundation of the world; but now, **once** at the end of the ages, He has appeared to put away sin by the sacrifice of Himself.

Jesus did this once! The Old Testament sacrifices were offered continuously for sin. The reason they were constantly offered was because they could not take away sin. They could only remind man of his sinful condition and the wages of sin – which is death. The insufficient sacrifice was offered again and again, but this is not so with Christ. If Christ's blood had to be applied again and again, the Bible says that He would have had to suffer again and again since the foundation of the world. But what actually happened? He put away sin completely by offering up Himself as a sacrifice for sin (singular). All sin was paid once and for all. It was sin, not sins.

The ordinance of confessing, sacrificing, and having sins covered was a yearly reminder that pointed to Christ. It was a foreshadow of what God was about to do. To turn away from Christ and back to what foreshadowed Him is now a sin. This Old Covenant ordinance was God's temporary provision to help His people understand Christ, but once the redemption came, to

Complete Redemption   45 return back to a system that denies Jesus' redemption is disbelief and is now sin. To understand this, look at **Hebrews 10:1-4**

> 1 For the law, having a shadow of the good things to come, *and* not the very image of the things, can never with these same sacrifices, which they offer continually year by year, make those who approach perfect.
> 2 For then would they not have ceased to be offered? For the worshipers, once purified, would have had no more consciousness of sins.
> 3 But in those *sacrifices there is* a reminder of sins every year.
> 4 For *it is* not possible that the blood of bulls and goats could take away sins.

Let's step back and analyze what has been said in this passage. First, the sacrifice that pointed to Christ could NEVER take away sin. Just as you and I are saved through Christ, the Old Testament saints are saved through Christ. They didn't obtain forgiveness through the law and the sacrifices it demanded. They are saved through faith in Christ, though they had to have faith in what had not yet been fully revealed.

Second, the perpetual repentance and sacrifice was offered because God required them to recognize that sin was still present and could not be removed. Instead of paying the penalty for sin, they transferred the wages of their sin to an animal who then was slain as a yearly reminder of the wages they deserved. It constantly reminded them that they were in bondage.

Third and the most important truth explained here is that the evidence that the sacrifice was insufficient to perfect them was that they still had the conscience of sin. If the sacrifice had been sufficient, their conscience should have been cleared. Not only cleared, but cleared to the point where they would not have to come back to the altar to seek forgiveness.

So this begs a few questions. First, is Jesus' sacrifice sufficient to take away sin? The obvious answer is 'Yes', for this is the entire focus of the New Testament. Second, if the reason the Old Testament saints had to keep visiting the altar and confessing their sins over the animal was because the sacrifice was insufficient and could not take away sin, then what should our response be to the sacrifice that was sufficient. If our sins are paid in Christ, sin has been taken away, and our conscience has been washed clean, isn't the perpetual revisitation of our sins and begging God for forgiveness at the altar a denial of Christ?

What are we trying to accomplish with perpetual confession of sin? What does the Bible tell us to confess?

If you look up confession in the Bible, those who do not know Christ are to confess their sins for the purpose of agreeing with God that they are sinners incapable of overcoming sin without a redeemer to pay the debt for them. From that point on, confession is always focused on Christ. The Bible says things like, "Hold fast to the confession of our hope without wavering,"[15] "We have a High Priest…Let us hold fast to our confession."[16] And what is our confession? It's found in **Romans 10:10-11**

[10] For with the heart one believes unto righteousness, and with the mouth confession is made unto salvation.
[11] For the Scripture says, "Whoever believes on Him will not be put to shame."

Your confession is not a declaration of the power of sin over your life. Your confession is belief in Jesus, who conquered your sin. That's why 1 John 2 tells us that the goal is that we do not sin, but if we do, we have an Advocate – Jesus Christ.

An advocate is a legal defender that pleads the innocence of his client. If Jesus is declaring that you are innocent, no one can call you guilty! And keep in mind that this is our focus when we DO sin. If anyone sins, we have an Advocate declaring we are innocent – Jesus Christ.

Do you believe in Jesus' declaration over you? Or do you believe the accuser who cries out your guilt, night and day? The Bible calls Satan our accuser, but his accusation has no merit in

---

[15] Hebrews 10:23
[16] Hebrews 4:14

heaven. He can only accuse you to yourself and other people who are looking at life through the flesh. In the fleshly mind, you will always feel your guilt. When you look to Christ, you will recognize His declaration of your innocence simply because you believe on Him.

Nowhere in the New Testament does God say, "Look at your sin." The Bible says that the mind set on the flesh will find death. And where does sin dwell? Sin is always an act of the flesh. So when someone says, "Look at your sin," they are telling you to take your eyes off Christ and fix your gaze on the flesh. If you look at yourself, you will always fall short. You will always be insufficient. You will always see flaws. There is only one way to be transformed into Christ's likeness, and that is to fix your eyes on Christ and trust in His power to defeat the weakness of your flesh.

Let's take a look at a few more passages. I want you to recognize the power of Christ's complete forgiveness. Now look at **Hebrews 7:26-27**

26 For such a High Priest was fitting for us, *who is* holy, harmless, undefiled, separate from sinners, and has become higher than the heavens;
27 who does not need daily, as those high priests, to offer up sacrifices, first for His own sins and then for the people's, for this He did once for all when He offered up Himself.

How many times did Jesus have to deal with sin? The earthly priest had to deal with his sin and then he would intercede for the people. Our High Priest, Jesus Christ, did not have His own sin to deal with. He offered Himself up for sin, once for all. Not when you blow it. Once for all. This is a common theme in the Bible and is again mentioned in **Hebrews 9:12**

Not with the blood of goats and calves, but with His own blood He entered the Most Holy Place once for all, having obtained eternal redemption.

This is a critical passage. In the Old Testament, the earthly high priest could only enter the holiest place of the temple once a year. He sprinkled the blood of the animal sacrifice on the altar as an offering for sin.

Jesus did not turn to the insufficient sacrifices that could only ease someone's conscience for a year. He took His own blood and ignored the earthly altar, but sprinkled the altar in heaven ONCE FOR ALL. The blood CANNOT be reapplied. It is sufficient, so it only had to happen once. Then all sin was removed and our redemption is eternal.

We aren't redeemed, slip back into slavery because we sin, and then need to be redeemed again. Our redemption is eternal. It's eternal because He didn't just deal with your past sins, or your individual sins. He took sin as a whole, defeated it, and redeemed you from all sin, once and for all. Do you believe?

When Jesus had an important teaching, He would say, "Truly (or verily) I say to you." If He repeated it twice, it was of critical importance. When something is repeated three times in the Bible, it is a foundational truth that is essential for us to understand the nature, character, or work of God. For the third time in three chapters, God is declaring the foundational principle that Jesus accomplished our forgiveness and redemption once and for all. Look at **Hebrews 10:10**

By that will we have been sanctified through the offering of the body of Jesus Christ once *for all.*

Do you suppose that God is trying to drive home the point that sin has been destroyed and taken out of the way? The work of Christ is not a perpetual act of confessing, getting forgiveness, and applying the blood of Christ to our lives? It was done once and for all, does not need to be redone, is not dependent upon our action, but is an eternal accomplishment that is complete and finished.

People have a hard time believing that Jesus did not merely deal with our past sins, but defeated sin as a whole. The noun sin has been destroyed so the verb (or action) of sin has no power. You were not freed from your past sins only to be subjugated by your future sins. You were freed from sin as a whole. Look now at **Romans 6:7-11**

7 For he who has died has been freed from sin.

8 Now if we died with Christ, we believe that we shall also live with Him,

9 knowing that Christ, having been raised from the dead, dies no more. Death no longer has dominion over Him.

10 For *the death* that He died, He died to sin once for all; but *the life* that He lives, He lives to God.

11 Likewise you also, reckon yourselves to be dead indeed to sin, but alive to God in Christ Jesus our Lord.

God set you free from sin by crucifying sin with Himself, and your flesh also with Himself. Your role is to believe, or reckon, yourself dead with Christ and dead to sin in the flesh, but alive for Christ in the Spirit. The flesh has no power over the Spirit, and once your old nature was taken away, all claims sin had against your life died with it. When your old nature died with Christ, you were set free from sin. Not merely sins, but sin as a whole. Nothing you do can give sin a claim over your eternal spirit.

Your old sinful nature was bound by sin. When it died, you were set free. Your new life is not subject to the bondage of sin, for the life born of the Spirit cannot be enslaved by the flesh or sin. In your body sin still wars against your mind, trying to bring you back into bondage,[17] but it cannot bring your life back into bondage. It can only persuade you to set your mind back into the flesh. But when you turn your focus to Christ, your mind is also free, and then walking in the Spirit is as natural to your new life as sin was to your old life.

Let's bring in a couple of other scriptures to sum up this chapter. Look at **Romans 6:18**

And having been set free from sin, you became slaves of righteousness.

Add to this **Romans 6:22**

---

[17] Romans 7:23

Complete Redemption

But now having been set free from sin, and having
become slaves of God, you have your fruit to holiness, and
the end, everlasting life.

Before you died with Christ and received a new nature of
God, you were slaves of sin. Sin, the noun, was a prison that
housed you. It kept you in bondage and its chains prevented you
from serving anything but itself.

Once you were set free from the prison of sin, you entered
the kingdom of righteousness. Just as your life was bound to sin
in the past, your life is now bound to righteousness. The wages
you earned in sin was death. The wages of the new life of
righteousness is everlasting life. You were chained to sin; now
you are bound to righteousness. One owner oppressed. Your
new master has adopted you as a child and heir of the kingdom.

The Old Testament gives word-pictures for this also. If a
slave loves his master, when his service is over, he has the
option of becoming a slave forever. The reason he would do this
is because his master treats him well and he recognizes that the
benefits of is slavery is better than life as a freeman. He would
then go through a ritual where he would be bound to that
master. Another Old Testament example is **Proverbs 29:21**

He who pampers his servant from childhood will have
him as a son in the end.

That is exactly what happens to a believer in Christ. We are
slaves of righteousness when we enter the Spirit by faith. We
recognize that being a slave of righteousness is a joy and not
oppression. We are treated as a son, and in the end, we are
adopted as sons as explained in **Romans 8:23**

We also who have the firstfruits of the Spirit, even we
ourselves groan within ourselves, eagerly waiting for the
adoption, the redemption of our body.

Our spirit is already a child of God. Our lives on this earth
are bound to righteousness, though it is still subject to the
temptations of this world. Yet in the end, when the fruit of the
Spirit of holiness has done its work, our fleshly bodies will be

changed and our adoption will be complete. We will inherit the kingdom as sons of God.

The Bible calls all believers sons of God, whether they are male or female. The reason is also a word-picture. The culture during the era of the Bible only allowed sons to inherit their father's possessions. Daughters married into someone else's inheritance. But with God, both men and women receive the inheritance and adoption as sons. There are not kings and queens in heaven. There are kings and priests, for all of us have the same inheritance regardless of our physical gender on earth.

You have been eternally redeemed. Your sins were not greater than the power of Christ before you were saved. They certainly cannot overcome the work of Christ after you are saved. Your weakness cannot defeat Christ's strength. Your sins cannot overcome the righteousness of God He has given to you.

The only power of sin in your life is your faith in sin's power. Temptation only has strength when you trust in its promises. You cannot overcome sin by confessing sin. You cannot overcome temptation by focusing on yourself. Here is your victory, **1 John 5:4-5**

> 4 For whatever is born of God overcomes the world. And this is the victory that has overcome the world-- our faith.
> 5 Who is he who overcomes the world, but he who believes that Jesus is the Son of God?

According to the Bible, you are already an overcomer. Sin may bluff you into submitting to it, but it only has the power of your faith in sin. If you struggle with sin or human weakness, what is the answer? Put your faith in Jesus Christ. This is your victory, faith in Christ. Believe that because you have been born again with a new spirit whose life is in God, you already have the victory that overcomes the world. Have faith in God.

Your confession of sin will never overcome sin. Begging God for re-forgiveness will not get you any more forgiven than you were when you came to Christ. It's time to stop trusting in the power of sin and start looking to the victory God has already accomplished for you. Confess Christ. Look to your advocate. Believe in the victory that has already overcome the world. Sin has no power over the Christian. Hold fast to your confession without wavering, and walk by faith in God's victory. Then you will discover what it means to be redeemed, and how you are already a victorious Christian.

God took sin out of the way so you can live by faith. You need not worry about sin. That's God's burden. You only need to focus on faith. Let's end with the promise given in the Old Testament that we now have in Christ, **Micah 7:19**

> He will again have compassion on us, And will subdue our iniquities. You will cast all our sins Into the depths of the sea.

Your sins are already buried in the sea of God's mercy. It cannot reemerge. What's more is that God has promised to subdue your iniquities.

Think about the power of this promise to you. You don't have to worry about sin because God has already washed it away. You don't have to worry about your sinful tendencies because it's God's responsibility to subdue your iniquities. Your only role is to walk by faith in His promises. He guards your heart from sin when you believe enough to trust Him.

If you exert yourself in trying to fix yourself, you are trying to overcome the flesh with the flesh. But the flesh doesn't have the promise of overcoming the world. Only faith has the promise of overcoming. When you are struggling with sin, weaknesses, or anything of the flesh, roll that care into God's hands. It's His job to carry that burden. You fix your eyes on the promise of life in Christ. Walk as the child of God you are, and let God produce the fruit of righteousness while He also subdues the sins and struggles that were once a hindrance.

It's all about faith. Walk by faith and you are already pleasing to God!

Discussion Questions

What is the difference between forgiveness and redemption?

Why can't a slave earn his way out of slavery?

Review Hebrews 7:27, Hebrews 9:12, Hebrews 9:26, Hebrews 9:28, and Hebrews 10:10. How many times does Jesus deal with sin or sins?

Read Hebrews 10:1-2. Why did the Old Testament people still have a consciousness of sin?

Is Jesus' sacrifice sufficient?

Does the worshipper need to keep coming to be purified if the sacrifice is sufficient to take away sin?

If our conscience still focuses on sin, are we trusting in Christ's completed work?

Why is Jesus called our Advocate? Can anyone challenge Jesus' advocacy on your behalf?

What is the difference between being a slave of sin and a slave of righteousness?

If a sinner does a good deed, does that change his nature into a righteous one?

If the righteous does an act of sin, does that transform his nature back into a sinful one?

How does the Christian overcome sin?

Review Micah 7:19. Explain what is our role in defeating sin and obtaining forgiveness.

Does God expect you to get your life right before you come to Him?

If a Christian falls into sin, what must they do?

The End of Wrath

Let's take a moment to review the difference between forgiveness and redemption. Forgiveness is to pardon someone from the penalty of breaking the law, but redemption is the payment of someone's debt.

For example, if a poor man steals to get money for his needs or wants, if he's caught, there are two areas of consequences. For breaking the law, there is a penalty. He could get jail time and have to serve as a prisoner for years. The second consequence is restitution. Going to jail does not eliminate the debt he owes to the one he robbed. Once out of jail, he still owes restitution, even if his time was served.

On the cross, Jesus accomplished both. The wages of sin and the debt to sin were both paid through Christ. The wages of sin is punishment and death. We are owed the wages of sin, but Jesus took the stripes for our iniquities and was bruised for our transgressions. He then died in our place. Not only that, but the Bible calls Jesus our Redeemer. He took our debt out of the way and set us free. He took our wages of sin, and paid our debt to the law. Both the punishment owed to us was laid upon Christ, and the debt we owed to the law was paid by Christ, thus leaving us free indeed.

Understanding this will help us to get a clearer picture of the gospel, and will help us to accurately interpret the scriptures. People often confuse forgiveness and redemption, and assume that when we sin, we are again indebted to the law. This is not possible, as we shall clearly see in the Bible.

The Bible says that the way of the cross is foolishness to those who are perishing. Scripture also teaches that the natural mind cannot receive or understand the ways of God, for they are spiritually discerned. In this we can gather two important truths. Those who are unredeemed and not born into the Spirit cannot grasp the truths of God. There is no way to explain doctrine to the lost soul – other than to teach them the invitation of Christ to take away their sins and give them new life.

There are many Christianized lost souls. They try to model their lives after the tenants of Christianity, but when it comes to living by the Spirit, they are unable to do so. They will then try to customize the Bible into a standard they can keep, try to drag other people down so they feel better about themselves, or they may give up on Christianity all together.

However, the warning that the natural mind cannot comprehend the things of the Spirit is not only to the unbeliever. When a Christian begins to look at faith through the flesh, it also will not make sense, for the carnal mind cannot receive the things of God. The way of faith can appear just as foolish to the true Christian as it is to the religious but lost church member, as it also will be to the non-religious world.

If a Christian tries to live for God by human effort, or begins to try to make sense of the Bible by anything other than faith in the Spirit, it will appear just as foolish as it is to the lost culture around us. A Christian can be just as fleshly (or carnal) minded as the world.

This is why the way of grace through faith is scoffed at by the church community. People often look at the Bible's teaching on grace and say things like, "If you believe that, you are justifying sin," or "grace / hypergrace will cause people to fall back into sin."

Can telling someone that sin has been defeated and cannot be again imputed against a Christian create a justification for sin? To the fleshly mind, yes. But to the mind in the Spirit, this is impossible. The real question is, "Is God telling the truth, or do we need to withhold the scriptures from the church out of fear that fleshly-minded people might try to manipulate God in their quest to justify sinning?" Sin that they are already committing with or without the knowledge of grace.

What we have done is replaced faith with a Christianized church law to protect people from sin, because we don't believe in the Spirit's power to transform us. We then teach people to trust in their ability to self-justify by the deeds of the law instead of trusting in God. We trust ourselves more than the power of the Spirit and call this faith.

Let me restate it this way. If we keep people in the flesh and use rules and fear to keep the church under control, are we any better than those whom Jesus condemned for their righteousness by personal effort? Will people sin if they are told sin cannot be imputed? Some indeed will sin. Yet, there is already sin in the church. Not only is sin rampant in the church, but rarely do we find a truly victorious Christian. We have congregations of infant Christians who are perpetually trying to reinter the faith as a newborn over and over again. The Apostle Paul criticized some of the early churches of this very thing. Look at **Hebrews 5:12**

> For though by this time you ought to be teachers, you
> need *someone* to teach you again the first principles of the
> oracles of God; and you have come to need milk and not
> solid food.

His complaint was that people in the church should have grown to the point of being disciple-makers, but they were still in need of learning the basics of the Christian life. And what was a roadblock in their way? The Bible tells us three verses later in **Hebrews 6:1**

> Therefore, leaving the discussion of the elementary
> *principles* of Christ, let us go on to perfection, not laying
> again the foundation of repentance from dead works and
> of faith toward God,

They were perpetually trying to lay again the foundation of repentance and not going on toward perfection. Their gaze was stuck on the dead works of the flesh so they could not see the invitation to walk by faith, where they were invited to draw closer to God. They were so focused on the flesh (including trying to repent of their own weaknesses) that they were not focusing on the Lord who redeemed and empowered them.

Many will argue that we must focus on our sins, perpetually repent, and keep begging for forgiveness. To help clear up this point of confusion, let's look at what the scriptures teach about sin. Let's begin in the Old Testament promise of Christ. Isaiah 53 explains that the wrath of God was laid upon

Christ and how He bore our sins so we could have peace with God. If you are not familiar with this, take a few moments to read Isaiah 53:2-6. Immediately after the promise of Christ removing our sins, the next chapter gives the results we receive. Look at **Isaiah 54:8-10**

> 8 With a little wrath I hid My face from you for a moment; But with everlasting kindness I will have mercy on you," Says the LORD, your Redeemer.
>
> 9 "For this *is* like the waters of Noah to Me; For as I have sworn That the waters of Noah would no longer cover the earth, So have I sworn That I would not be angry with you, nor rebuke you.
>
> 10 For the mountains shall depart And the hills be removed, But My kindness shall not depart from you, Nor shall My covenant of peace be removed," Says the LORD, who has mercy on you.

Through the law, we were separated from God. He hid His face for a moment so man could recognize his condition and what was missing when mankind trusts in his own righteousness. The penalty of the law took us into judgment so we could look up from our despair and find the offering of mercy. Then to those who recognize their need, they enter into a new life where God has both removed sin, and the law that condemned us for our sin. Let's look at the end of the law for the Christian by beginning with **Colossians 2:13-14**

> 13 And you, being dead in your trespasses and the uncircumcision of your flesh, He has made alive together with Him, having forgiven you all trespasses,
>
> 14 having wiped out the handwriting of requirements that was against us, which was contrary to us. And He has taken it out of the way, having nailed it to the cross.

In an earlier chapter we looked at Colossians when it talked about the circumcision made without hands, where God's Spirit cut out our fleshly nature and we were born again with a new nature. This is also affirmed in **2 Corinthians 5:17**

Therefore, if anyone *is* in Christ, *he is* a new creation; old things have passed away; behold, all things have become new.

Your old nature passed away and a new nature has been created in you. There is much to teach on the new spirit we have received, but that will be for another study. What's important now is to understand that our old nature died, was buried with Christ, and passed away. We now are a new creation with a new nature and everything has become new.

Not only was our sinful nature cut away with the circumcision of the Spirit and nailed to the cross, but look closely at Colossians above. Not only was our sins and old nature removed, but so was the law that condemned us. The handwriting of the law, which was not for us but was contrary to us, has been taken out of the way and nailed to the cross.

This makes the promise of Isaiah clearer. How can God our Redeemer say that just as the promise to Noah was sure, His promise of the new covenant is just as sure. He has declared as an oath that cannot be broken, "I will not be angry with you nor rebuke you again." God has put Himself under an unbreakable covenant oath that His wrath is off the table. Never again will you be rebuked and placed back under the wrath due to sin. Why? Because the law does not apply to the new creation. It only applies to those outside of Christ.

Here is a great point of confusion. People who trust in their own ability to fulfill the law (which has only happened once in history when Jesus accomplished all things) get upset when the law is challenged. I had someone confront me with the words of Jesus. He said, "Jesus said that even if heaven and earth should pass away, the law will never pass away." Not so. Jesus said it would not pass away until all the law has been fulfilled.[18] This was NOT a call for you and me to fulfill it, but it was Jesus declaring His soon to be completed work. He even says as much in **Matthew 5:17**

---

[18] Matthew 5:18

Do not think that I came to destroy the Law or the Prophets. I did not come to destroy but to fulfill.

Now you are a fulfiller of the law because of your faith in what Christ has accomplished for you. This is explained in **Romans 8:1-4**

> 1 *There is* therefore now no condemnation to those who are in Christ Jesus, who do not walk according to the flesh, but according to the Spirit.
> 2 For the law of the Spirit of life in Christ Jesus has made me free from the law of sin and death.
> 3 For what the law could not do in that it was weak through the flesh, God *did* by sending His own Son in the likeness of sinful flesh, on account of sin: He condemned sin in the flesh,
> 4 that the righteous requirement of the law might be fulfilled in us who do not walk according to the flesh but according to the Spirit.

The righteous requirement of the law has been FULFILLED in you if you are in the Spirit. Is this a conditional statement? The only condition is to be in Christ. Look a few verses later in **Romans 8:9**

> But you are not in the flesh but in the Spirit, if indeed the Spirit of God dwells in you. Now if anyone does not have the Spirit of Christ, he is not His.

There is only one requirement for the law – faith in Christ. If you are in Christ, you are in the Spirit. You may not walk according to the Spirit, but this does not change the fact that your life is hid in Christ and you are a spiritual man or woman. Most Christians are ignorant of this truth and walk according to the flesh, but we are called to walk by faith.

Believe God's word! You HAVE fulfilled the law because you are in the Spirit if you are in Christ. If you are not in Christ, the law stands as your accuser with all its penalties and consequences. Yet, God so loved the world that He gave Christ as the provision of sin. Any who believe on Him will not perish, but have everlasting life.[19] Look also at **Romans 8:2**

> For the law of the Spirit of life in Christ Jesus has made me free from the law of sin and death.

You are under the law of faith[20] and the law of the Spirit of life. You are not under the law of sin and death, nor are you under the law that demands your righteousness. When the Galatian church was persuaded to turn back and put themselves under the law, the Apostle Paul said, "You who desire to be under the law, do you not hear the law?" He then goes on to explain that the Old Testament gives a word picture of Ismael, who was born of a woman in bondage, and Isaac, who was born into God's promise. The child of the bondwoman was cast out so he could not inherit the promise.

The Bible then goes on to explain that those under the law brought down from Mount Sinai by Moses are the children of bondage, but we are the children of promise. This explanation was given in response to Jewish Christians who were trying to teach new believers that they had to keep the law – not just believe in Christ for salvation.

So why would the children of promise want to join those under the law of bondage, where there is no promise? Yet, there is a growing movement in the church to return to the law. There are those who again teach that a Christian can only be blessed if they keep the law, the feast days, Sabbath days, or any number of ways we can submit back under the law of bondage. The truth is that a Christian is forfeiting their life of promise by believing they must return to the law. Or as the Bible explains in **Romans 10:3-4**

> 3 For they being ignorant of God's righteousness, and seeking to establish their own righteousness, have not submitted to the righteousness of God.
> 4 For Christ *is* the end of the law for righteousness to everyone who believes.

---

[19] John 3:16
[20] Romans 3:27

You cannot seek your own righteousness and submit to God's righteousness at the same time. Christ is not only the end of the law of sin and death as we read earlier, but He is also the end of the law for righteousness to you who believe. You receive His righteousness by faith. Righteousness is not what you do. It is God's gift to you. You are the righteousness of God in Christ. Your attempts at becoming righteous is actually rebellion against faith. It is the flesh masquerading as Christ.

Christians who submit back under the law have stepped outside of God's promise that He will never again be angry and will never again rebuke us. God still is not placing wrath upon the believer, but the law stands as an accuser to those under the law. This is why so many Christians are afraid of judgment and feel as if they are under condemnation.

God said, "There is therefore no condemnation to those who are in Christ," but those under the law can no longer see the promise. They can only see the judgment of the law. That's also why the Bible says that when the law is read, a veil is over their eyes and they remain blind until they turn to Christ. [21]

But to those who are focused on Christ and have faith in the promise, they are free, sin is not imputed, and the Spirit transforms the actions of our outer man into agreement with the nature of our inner man. Consider the promise of **Romans 4:7-8**

> [7] "Blessed *are those* whose lawless deeds are forgiven,
> And whose sins are covered;
> [8] Blessed *is the* man to whom the LORD shall not impute sin."

Are you blessed? If you are in the promise of God, this is given as your assurance. Not only are you blessed because your past sins are forgiven, but you are double blessed because God will NOT impute sin to you.

This passage makes the legalistic mind squirm. Yet, it can't be denied. It doesn't say, blessed is the one who does not sin. It

---

[21] 2 Corinthians 3:14

says, "Blessed is the man whom the Lord shall not impute sin." You are imputed with Christ's righteousness. Keep reading in Romans 4 and you'll see the promise that God is imputing His righteousness to you.

We know the above scripture is talking about our own sin, for God has stated that people are only held accountable for their own sins.[22] The promise is that when you sin, because you are in Christ, your sin will not be imputed to you, and therefore you are called Blessed of the Lord! Why is this true? Look at **Romans 5:13**

> For until the law sin was in the world, but sin is not imputed when there is no law.

So does this mean there are no consequences and that I can sin freely? Read the full chapter of Romans 5. Sin was in the world causing death, disease, oppression, and sorrow.

When sin is exalted, it produces death. So indeed there are consequences, but those consequences are limited to the life in the flesh. Plus the Bible says that whatever someone sows, they will reap. You can sow in the flesh and harvest the things of the flesh. You can invest your life into the very things that caused you pain and create sorrow in the world today. Certainly you can invest your life in the way of death, but you cannot nullify the work of Christ.

If you believe your sin could overcome the victory of Christ, you have lowered Christ to a human standard. The truth is that you cannot defeat the work of Christ. You can only build your life upon faith, or upon the flesh. You can reap the things of spiritual life, or the things of death. But you cannot defeat God!

In the next chapter we'll discuss sin in the Christian's life and how we overcome, but don't exalt sin over Christ. Don't deny the word of God because your human understanding can't grasp why God's grace is not nullified by sin. Don't deny the truth that the law has passed away through Christ. To affirm this truth even more, let's begin wrapping this chapter up by looking at **2 Corinthians 3:7-8**

---

[22] Deuteronomy 24:16

⁷ But if the ministry of death, written *and* engraved on stones, was glorious, so that the children of Israel could not look steadily at the face of Moses because of the glory of his countenance, which *glory* was passing away,

⁸ how will the ministry of the Spirit not be more glorious?

The law had glory. Yet its glory was limited because it depended upon the flesh, or as the Bible says, the weakness of the law was the flesh.[23] According to the Bible, the glory of the law was passing away as the glory of the ministry of the Spirit emerged. The law must decrease that grace may increase. The law brought us to Christ, but then had to decrease in submission to the glory of what it pointed to.

We see a great example of this in the last Old Testament prophet, John the Baptist. He was the prophet that had the privilege of delivering God's people, who were under the law to the new covenant of Christ.

Jesus made an interesting statement about John the Baptist in Matthew 11:11. He said there was no greater prophet than John the Baptist, but the least person in the Kingdom of God was greater than John.

Until I understood grace, this did not make sense to me. First of all, how could John be the greatest prophet? What about those great miracle working prophets, Elijah and Elisha? Why is John greater than these? And how could he be the greatest prophet, but lesser than the lowest person in the Kingdom of God?

To help understand this, let's go back to Moses and Joshua. Moses was the lawgiver, and Joshua was the picture of Christ. Moses could not enter into the Promised Land. He had to decrease and die so Joshua could take over and lead the people into the promise. In the same way, John was the prophet that took the people to the promise, then decreased as he gave up his authority to Jesus. John, the representative of the law had to decrease and die so the Promise-giver could increase and bring in the new covenant.

---

[23] Romans 8:3

The End of Wrath

John was the greatest prophet because he delivered the people into the New Covenant. He had the privilege of doing the thing that all the other prophets desired to see but never saw. He is the only prophet who was able to point the people to Christ and say, "Behold the Lamb of God, who takes away the sin of the world."

He was the greatest prophet because he delivered the Old Covenant into the New Covenant. Yet, he was lesser than the least in God's kingdom because he was still under the law. The greatest prophet was still unredeemed. He still had an old nature. He had a great calling and the gift of a prophet, but he didn't have the gift of sonship, and could not become a child of God under the law. He was a slave to sin and the law, not a son of promise. He died as a natural man. Just as all the prophets before him, he died waiting for his sins to be taken away in Christ. As with all the other Old Testament saints, he will pass through Christ into salvation through faith in what was yet to come, but those who received Christ had a gift that was incomparable to what the Old Covenant saints had.

Not one prophet was called a son of God. Not one prophet had the privilege of coming boldly before the throne of grace. Not one prophet entered the holiest place of the temple. The holiest place was off limits until the veil of the temple was torn by God from the top to the bottom. God exposed the most sacred place that was once reserved for Him alone, and opened it to everyone who will come through Christ.

Through Christ, we have a right to go where no prophet ever went. We have unlimited access to God's holiest place, while the Old Covenant high priests could only visit once a year. And they NEVER had the ability to approach the throne with confidence.

We have the invitation by God – no, the command of God – to come boldly before God's throne for help when we are in need (not when we feel perfected). The high priest had to perform many cleansing rituals and fulfill every ordinance. Even then, the other priests tied a rope to his leg and bells on his clothing in case he was struck down for his sins. If the bells stopped making noise, they knew he was found guilty by God and the rope was the only way to pull him out. No one else was allowed into the holiest place of the temple.

The least person in God's kingdom has the temple of God within them. Each person has fellowship with God that cannot be broken. In Christ, we have the promise that judgment cannot fall upon us. We have the purification that no prophet ever received. Not one prophet had God's Spirit within them. The Spirit came upon them, but never indwelled them. Yet the prophets had the honor of pointing to our day, and declaring the promise that we now have. Look at **Ezekiel 36:26**

> I will give you a new heart and put a new spirit within
> you; I will take the heart of stone out of your flesh and
> give you a heart of flesh.

They hoped for this day, but we have this now. When we are born into God's kingdom, God takes away the corrupted heart of flesh that was hardened by sin and gives us a new heart that is tender toward Him. He then gives us a new spirit that is born of God *and* puts His Holy Spirit within us. We now have continuous fearless fellowship with the very God that the Old Testament saints feared.

They could not approach God, but now He abides within us. They were afraid of God, we have joy in our intimate fellowship with God. They had to sacrifice because their sins were ever present. We have had our sins removed. They had to learn the law as they tried in vain to make their flesh go against its nature. We now learn of God so we can learn to walk according to our new nature that is already in harmony with God.

Trusting in God and cultivating our relationship born out of God's agape love (which is grace) does not create sin. It helps us to walk in victory – a victory that can never be accomplished through the law or any human effort.

Discussion Question

If we don't believe living by grace through faith can create victory over sin, can keeping the law through human effort do better?

Why does the Bible call 'laying again the foundation of repentance' the elementary things of God?

How do we leave this behind and go on toward perfection?

Review Isaiah 54:8-10. Read Romans 5:9, and 1 Thessalonians 5:9. Why does God promise to never again be angry or have wrath against His people?

Is the promise to Noah against another flood conditional upon man's ability not to sin? What about the New Covenant?

Review again Isaiah 53:10. How many sins does it take to nullify this promise?

How does Colossians 2:13-14 apply to the Christian's life?

If the law that condemned us was taken out of the way, what condemns us when we blow it?

Review Romans 8:4. Have you fulfilled the law? Explain.

Review Romans 10:4. Has the law come to an end for the Christian?

Read Romans 4:7-8. Are Christians blessed? Are our sins forgiven? Does God impute sin or righteousness?

Can your sin defeat the work of Christ? Explain.

Why did Jesus call John the Baptist the greatest prophet?

Why is the least person in the Kingdom of God (the New Covenant) greater than John?

What does the least person in the Kingdom have that the prophets and Old Testament saints did not have?

Overcoming Sin

John 1:29

> The next day John saw Jesus coming toward him, and said, "Behold! The Lamb of God who takes away the sin of the world!"

Jesus did not merely come to suppress sin, but to make an end of it. Sin was defeated in Christ, and any who are in Christ have been freed from sin. Romans 6:7 concludes that since we were buried with Christ and have died to our old life when we were born again, "He who has died has been freed from sin." The church does not believe this biblical truth, even though it is consistently taught throughout the New Testament. Let's also bring in **Hebrews 9:26**

> He then would have had to suffer often since the foundation of the world; but now, once at the end of the ages, He has appeared to put away sin by the sacrifice of Himself.

Jesus took away sin, and all who are in Christ are under Jesus' victory over sin. Sin was defeated, but instead of preaching the defeat of sin, the church teaches that we are still under the power of sin. If the church was as obsessed with righteousness as it is about sin, the average Christian would be experiencing the benefits of spiritual maturity, instead of trusting in Satan's power through sin.

I'm going to tell you something few Christians have ever heard in church but is something I wish someone had taught me. It's not your job to overcome sin. It's not your job to overcome your weaknesses. It's your job to believe God's word and allow the Spirit to transform you into spiritual maturity. There is a reason why the Bible calls all the attributes of Christian maturity 'the Fruit of the Spirit'.

Fruit is not something that comes through labor. I've never observed a grapevine grunting and straining to produce grapes.

Fruit is the natural result of what happens when the life of the vine flows into the branches. The branches do nothing but rest and grow. Growth is not an act of labor. It's something that cannot be rushed, nor can it be regulated. Either the vine is healthy or it is defective. Cut off the life and the vine dies. Even a cut branch will grow if it is grafted back into the vine.

Take to heart the words of Jesus in **John 15:4-5**

> 4 "Abide in Me, and I in you. As the branch cannot bear fruit of itself, unless it abides in the vine, neither can you, unless you abide in Me.
>
> 5 "I am the vine, you *are* the branches. He who abides in Me, and I in him, bears much fruit; for without Me you can do nothing.

A fruitful life is a guarantee to those who trust in Christ. The role of a disciple is to learn to abide in Christ – the source of our life and power in the Spirit. What Christians don't seem to realize is that the flesh is not a hindrance to our spiritual life. It's the other way around. The flesh emerges when our spiritual life is lacking. It cannot overcome our life in the Spirit.

Just as darkness can NEVER drive light out of a room, the flesh can NEVER drive the light of your life in Christ out of its rightful place. Darkness is the absence of light and the flesh is the absence of the Spirit.

Before you were born into the Spirit, you had nothing but the flesh. The flesh will exalt itself through either blatant sins, or through spiritual looking acts that can feed the ego of the flesh and its desire to declare its own righteousness. Ultimately the flesh reigns because the life of the Spirit is absent.

So what happens when a Christian neglects God's invitation to walk by faith? The flesh takes the reins. The fleshly minded Christian can overcome certain habits, but only if there is something else fleshly to take its place. But when the flesh feels deprived, we fall back to what comforts it. Sometimes that comfort is in destructive or sinful habits.

The flesh troubles our lives because it has taken a stronghold in the absence of a healthy spirit. And herein lies the struggle of the Christian. Most church teaching does more to empower the flesh than to mature our spirit.

When a preacher calls from the pulpit, "Look at your sin," where is the mind focused? If I am focused on sin, then I am setting my mind on the things of the flesh, and the Bible clearly says the mind set on the flesh is death. The mind on the Spirit is life. We think we must wrestle against sin, but this is false. We are called to turn away from sin and toward Christ. We are not told to grovel in the shame of sin, but to obey the words of **Hebrews 4:16**

> Let us therefore come boldly to the throne of grace, that we may obtain mercy and find grace to help in time of need.

When we are weak and tempted, and when we have blown it and have been defeated by the flesh, God *commands* us to come boldly to the throne of grace that we may obtain help when we are in need. Grace means unmerited and unearned favor. God has commanded that when you sin, boldly come before His throne of favor to receive more favor when you need help in your weaknesses. Not judgment, but favor. And here is the favor we can expect. Look at a passage we studied earlier, **Micah 7:19**

> He will again have compassion on us, And will subdue our iniquities. You will cast all our sins Into the depths of the sea.

God delights in compassion. This was an Old Testament foretelling of the New Testament promise. We are now in that promise through Christ. Your sins have already been cast into the depths of the sea. God's throne of grace is the place where compassion is always given. An important promise found in this passage applies to our discussion. It is God, not you, who subdues your iniquities!

The sins that plague you in the flesh are defeated when you put your trust in God's throne of grace. Yet if you are in disbelief, you will believe the lie that you must get your life right in order to become acceptable again. It's a twofold lie. First, you are accepted in the Beloved (Christ). If Christ is accepted by your heavenly Father, then you are accepted. Therefore, anyone who teaches that you are no longer acceptable to God is teaching that sin is greater than Christ, and they are denying God's declaration that Christ has made you completely accepted.

The second part of that lie is that you can do nothing to make yourself acceptable to God. Nothing you can do will make God accept you other than faith in Christ. Those who think they must do something to get it right are trusting in their own works instead of Christ's.

We all have weaknesses of the flesh. When we allow our minds to return to the flesh, or we neglect our life in the Spirit, the flesh will take advantage of the void we've created, and take ground for its own purposes.

Some teach that we must do certain things to regain the stronghold and take back our lives for God. There is even a teaching that we are under a generational curse that can only be broken when WE do things to make God accept us. It is often taught that we must find out and confess the sins of our fathers and forefathers. We can't even recognize most of our own sins, so how can we have any hope of confessing the sins of our forefathers? It's not only the 'big sins' that are part of the curse.

The generational curse does not exist and never did. This is a misinterpretation of the scripture where God warned the nation of Israel that the nation would be judged up to four generations if they turned from God to follow other gods. Yet in the same passages God said, "The children will not be judged for the sins of their fathers, nor the fathers for their children."

Even if there had been a generational curse, that curse was broken in Christ. Galatians 3:13 tells us that Jesus redeemed us from the curse of the law by becoming a curse for us. The only curse placed upon man was the curse of the law. The only way a Christian can be cursed is to return to the law. Galatians 3:10a says:

For as many as are of the works of the law are under the curse...

The law is the curse. There is no curse to those who are in Christ. Yet, we do have to contend with a flesh that is still corrupted by sin. As I stated previously, the flesh cannot be defeated by you. God has reserved this victory solely for Himself, and you are victorious in Him. Take to heart the words of **Romans 8:13**

> For if you live according to the flesh you will die; but if by the Spirit you put to death the deeds of the body, you will live.

How are the sinful deeds of the body of flesh overcome? It's not you that overcomes. It is the Spirit, and you are an overcomer when you trust in the Spirit. Sin may indeed defeat you (and it will do so often) until you learn to walk by faith. But this isn't your concern. It's God's job to suppress your iniquities and put to death the deeds of the body by His Holy Spirit.

The truth is that you are already an overcomer in Christ, but that victory doesn't become reality in your life until you receive it by faith. Not faith in your ability to measure up to God through religion. It is faith in Christ and the promise of the Spirit. If you are in Christ, you have already overcome, but that victory is not experienced outside of faith – which is how we walk in the Spirit. Look at the amazing promise of **1 John 5:4-5**

> 4 For whatever is born of God overcomes the world. And this is the victory that has overcome the world-- our faith.
> 5 Who is he who overcomes the world, but he who believes that Jesus is the Son of God?

According to the Bible, when you receive Christ, you are born of God with a new spirit. In the Spirit, you have already overcome, but there is only one way to experience that victory in daily life – faith. To clarify it further, the Bible explains that faith is believing in Jesus Christ.

Jesus said, "Be of good cheer, for I have overcome the world."[24] He overcame, and when you trust in Him, you have overcome through Him. Your body of flesh is part of this fallen

---

[24] John 16:33

Overcoming Sin

world, but your spirit is not. It has been born of God and cannot sin. Look at **1 John 3:9**

Whoever has been born of God does not sin, for His seed remains in him; and he cannot sin, because he has been born of God.

Add to this **1 Peter 1:23**

Having been born again, not of corruptible seed but incorruptible, through the word of God which lives and abides forever,

Your new nature is a gift of God, was born of God, has its life in God, and always remains in God. It has to be incorruptible, for if our spirit could sin, we would become incompatible with God again, just as was the case when we were under the sinful nature of Adam.

This is important to understand, because if we think our sins corrupt our spirit, we can never have the confidence to come boldly to God's throne. We will also be approaching the Christian life from a fleshly minded perspective. We'll be trying to use our behavior to create spiritual acceptance, instead of looking to the Spirit to bring our bodies under subjection.

Overcoming cannot be attained from the outside in. We can't force our behavior to transform our minds, and our minds to mature our spirit. No, it's our spirit that reveals the mind of Christ to our understanding, which then begins to transform our behavior.

If you try to change yourself through forced behavior modification, you will be discouraged and frustrated when you struggle, and it will do nothing to create spiritual maturity. However, if you grow in Christ, your outward behavior will begin to transform into agreement with your inward life.

Why is sin tempting? We are tempted when we have an unmet need that we believe sin can satisfy. When there is a spiritual emptiness in our heart, we hunger for satisfaction, and that is when Satan points us to sin with the false promise that we can be satisfied outside of Christ. To the soul that is filled with the spirit, there is no lack, and temptation loses its appeal. Or as **Proverbs 27:7** states:

> A satisfied soul loathes the honeycomb, But to a hungry soul every bitter thing *is* sweet.

The bitterness of sin appears sweet to the starving soul, but the promise of temptation is loathsome to the one fed by the Spirit. There are countless Christians that believe the Spirit can't satisfy, because they have never been taught the power of walking in the Spirit. To combat temptation, instead of directing believers to be filled with the Spirit as the Bible instructs, the church is being directed to the emptiness of life in the law, and trying to use fear and guilt to shame people into resisting temptation.

A life that discovers grace is satisfied in Christ, and needs no law, guilt, or fear to fight off temptation. Temptation becomes irrelevant to the one who is full. It's only the life that neglects the Spirit that feels the drawing of temptation.

When you sin, it's the evidence that your mind is in the flesh. The mind in the flesh cannot please God, and this is true whether your fleshly behavior is religious or rebellious. Sin is always in the body of flesh, but it has no power unless our minds are in the flesh where sin dwells. The Bible gives a great explanation of this in **Romans 7:17-23**

> 17 But now, *it is* no longer I who do it, but sin that dwells in me.
> 18 For I know that in me (that is, in my flesh) nothing good dwells; for to will is present with me, but *how* to perform what is good I do not find.
> 19 For the good that I will *to do*, I do not do; but the evil I will not *to do*, that I practice.
> 20 Now if I do what I will not *to do*, it is no longer I who do it, but sin that dwells in me.
> 21 I find then a law, that evil is present with me, the one who wills to do good.
> 22 For I delight in the law of God according to the inward man.
> 23 But I see another law in my members, warring against

the law of my mind, and bringing me into captivity to the law of sin which is in my members.

There is much to glean from this passage. The first thing to note is that twice the Apostle Paul says, "It is no longer I who do it, but sin that dwells in me." He says 'no longer' because when he was unredeemed, he had a dead spirit that was sinful by nature. Before Christ, it was 'I' who sinned. After Christ, it is my willful actions behaving in a way that is contrary to who I am. The new nature does not sin, but as stated in verse 18, in our flesh, nothing good dwells.

Verse 23 explains that sin dwells in our body of flesh and still craves to be gratified. In order to satisfy that craving, the flesh wars to attempt to regain control of our minds so we serve the sin that still remains in the flesh. If you go on to read the next few verses, Paul cries out, "Who will save me from this body of sin and death," but then answers that question with his declaration of victory. It is through Christ. Look at **Romans 7:25**

I thank God-- through Jesus Christ our Lord! So then, with the mind I myself serve the law of God, but with the flesh the law of sin.

This is a very important passage, for it is the battle every Christian faces. If you try to serve God through the flesh, you are still serving sin. The flesh can do nothing other than to serve the law of sin. But with the mind set on the Spirit, you serve the law of God. Serving the law of God is as natural to the mind in the Spirit as sin is to the body of flesh.

The very next passage declares that there is no condemnation to those who are in Christ. This promise is given as encouragement to us who are struggling with the flesh warring and sometimes temporarily gaining control of our minds to serve sin.

If we don't understand this battle, Satan will beat us down with condemnation, and tempt us into warring in the flesh, falsely believing that we can eventually make the flesh serve God. And when it does not, we are stuck in a perpetual cycle of defeat. Let's step back a couple of chapters in Romans to bring in a few verses that help clarify this. Look at **Romans 6:5-7**

> 5 For if we have been united together in the likeness of His death, certainly we also shall be *in the likeness* of *His* resurrection,
>
> 6 knowing this, that our old man was crucified with *Him*, that the body of sin might be done away with, that we should no longer be slaves of sin.
>
> 7 For he who has died has been freed from sin.

Begin from the stated promise that you have been freed from sin. It no longer controls you or has a claim over your life. You are free. Let's reiterate that again. You are free. If sin had any power over you, the Bible could not say you have been freed from sin. Not 'will be', but 'have been' freed from sin.

This means that from the point you are born into the Spirit by faith in Christ, sin has been defeated and you are no longer under sin's power. You can never again be enslaved by sin. You can submit to it, but it still has no power. Only your trust in sin gives it any power, though its strength is a mirage and not reality.

At the moment you trusted in Christ, your old man (or old nature) was crucified with Christ, buried with Christ, and is dead and gone. You DO NOT have two natures. You had one nature, a sinful one. Now you still have one nature, the new man born of God and incorruptible.

This is necessary to understand because when your old nature was crucified, it broke the power of sin. If you had two natures, this could not be said.

There is a little bit lost in translation in this passage. Some translations say, 'the body of sin was destroyed,' and the New King James I quoted here says, 'done away with.' This phrase comes from a single Greek word 'katargeo' which literally means 'unemployed'.

Knowing this meaning helps us to understand why one passage seems to say that the body of sin is gone, while two chapters later we are told sin in our body is the cause of the sin that wars against our minds.

Before Christ, our flesh ruled our minds because it was employed by our old sinful nature. Once our sinful nature was crucified with Christ and taken out of the way, our flesh was unemployed and rendered powerless. It no longer has a sinful nature to rule us; therefore when the body craves sin, it must war against our minds and try to bring us under its employment so we serve sin through the body.

When we sin, we have not lost the love or acceptance of God. We have allowed our minds to be in the flesh, and once our minds are fleshly thinking, we'll become fleshly acting. Yet the answer is not to grovel in the flesh, but to set our minds back in the Spirit.

How does one have the mind in the Spirit? To walk in the Spirit means to walk by faith and to think by faith. Here is a good example of a mind in faith. Look at **Romans 8:37-39**

37 Yet in all these things we are more than conquerors through Him who loved us.

38 For I am persuaded that neither death nor life, nor angels nor principalities nor powers, nor things present nor things to come,

39 nor height nor depth, nor any other created thing, shall be able to separate us from the love of God which is in Christ Jesus our Lord.

The mind stuck in the flesh says, "I am no longer accepted because I have sinned." The mind in faith says, "Nothing can separate me from God's love. I am more than a conqueror because of Christ."

You weren't righteous because of what you did before you sinned. Nor can your sin defeat the righteousness of God given to you. Unbelief looks at sin and is persuaded to deny that God's grace is sufficient to overcome our weakness. Faith believes when God said He delights in those who hope in His mercy, who come boldly to grace when in need; and who believe that God's righteousness can overcome sin.

A man or woman of faith understands that sinful habits are broken by trusting God's promise to subdue our sins, trusts the promise that the Spirit puts to death the deeds of the body, and that Jesus pleads our innocence even when we sin. The fleshly mind says, "Grace is nullified when I sin. Otherwise, I will be getting away with it. Grace will only make me want to sin."

Faith says, "Unbelief is what causes me to sin but grace teaches me to deny ungodliness and teaches me to live righteously."[25]

You cannot overcome sin by focusing on sin. You can't become righteous by focusing on your own righteousness. Sin is defeated when you reckon yourself dead indeed to sin but alive to God in Christ.[26] To reckon is to believe something God has said is true. Your eyes of the flesh looks at your performance and disbelieves the word of God. Eyes of faith looks at the multifaceted gift of grace and believes in its reality, even when the flesh gets the upper hand for a moment.

The truth is that your flesh won't lose its grip until you learn to walk by faith. The more you grow in faith, the less temptation will haunt you. Sins that once seemed undefeatable will fade away without you having to force yourself into self-control. Self-control is the fruit of the Spirit, so it becomes the natural growth of the life lived by faith.

It's time to stop focusing on yourself and begin to believe what God has declared about you. Nowhere in the Bible does God say you will overcome if you worry about sin. Nowhere does He say to try harder or become righteous for Him. It's all about trusting in His transforming power. Let's end this chapter with **2 Corinthians 3:17-18**

17 Now the Lord is the Spirit; and where the Spirit of the Lord *is*, there *is* liberty.

18 But we all, with unveiled face, beholding as in a mirror the glory of the Lord, are being transformed into the same image from glory to glory, just as by the Spirit of the Lord.

If you read this entire chapter, the veiled face is the person who is blinded by the law. The one who tries to become acceptable to God by human effort is blinded to the liberty we

---

25 Titus 2:11-12
26 Romans 6:11

have in Christ, and the power He has to transform us without human effort or limitations of the flesh.

You have liberty because you are free from the burden of the law, freed from sin, and freed from the weakness of the flesh. And how are you transformed into Christ's likeness? By looking at Christ. The more you have eyes of faith to see the promise of grace, the more you see His glory in you.

When we looked at the law, it reflected our sin, guilt, and condemnation to us. This is because the law was dependent upon man. When we look at grace, it becomes the mirror that reveals Christ's glory back to us. As we behold Christ, we see it as a mirror, and the more we behold Him, the more we discover the image of Christ placed within us by the Holy Spirit.

We are then transformed into His likeness because we are learning to recognize who we are in Him. His Spirit is within us, and as we look to Him, we find He is in us, and we in Him. The more this reality is unveiled in our minds, the more we will allow it to transform our outward lives into what we understand is truly our life in Christ.

Examining yourself cannot do this. Looking at your sin and failure cannot transform you. The more you study your failures, the more you transform your behavior back toward the flesh. But the more you behold Christ, the more you am transformed into the person you are in Him!

Do you see the truth of this principle? The more you behold the flesh and your failures, the more you are transformed into the flesh. The more you behold Christ, the more you are transformed into the image of God. Your outward behavior is a reflection of where you are focused.

Focusing on your sin produces more sin. Focusing on grace cannot produce sin. It eliminates sin, for as you grow into who you are in Christ, sin has no place to abide. It cannot abide in the light, and in Christ, there is no shadow of turning. This is the ONLY way to defeat sin in your life. Best of all, it's the work of God and is His gift to you. You have been given the gift of grace!

Discussion Questions

What does the Bible mean when it says Jesus took away the sin of the world?

Read part of Paul's testimony in Acts 26:17-18. Also read Romans 10:10-11. When do we experience the removal of sin?

Review Micah 7:19. What is our role in overcoming sin? What is God's role?

Read Galatians 5:16. How do we overcome lustful desires?

If we have given into sin, does this prevent us from walking in the Spirit?

Why does temptation seem appealing?

Why does 1 John 3:9 tell us that we cannot sin?

Review Romans 7:17-23. Where is sin dwell according to the Bible?

How do we overcome?

Does Romans 7:17 and 1 John 3:9 help you to understand why Christians struggle and how we overcome?

Do you have to stop sinning before you can begin growing spiritually?

Read Romans 7:25, 8:1, and 8:9. If you sin, are you back under condemnation?

Do you still have a sin nature? Why or why not?

Does the Bible tell us to become righteous for Him?

How are we transformed into Christ's likeness?

How does our outward behavior reflect where we are focused?

The Purpose of Sin

Anytime grace is taught as the Bible presents it, this question almost always comes up. I've never had anyone say that the scriptures I've presented in this book are not saying what they appear to be saying. Instead, people fall back to human reasoning and say, "If that's true, people will feel justified in sin and will sin more." Let's answer this objection with **Proverbs 3:5-6**

> 5 Trust in the LORD with all your heart, And lean not on your own understanding;
>
> 6 In all your ways acknowledge Him, And He shall direct your paths.

As stated previously, the ways of God seem foolish to the natural mind. How can sin be completely removed, once and for all, and it not cause us to rejoice in sin?

What people are actually saying is, "I don't believe God has given us a new nature, and I don't believe the Spirit has the power to transform us without intimidating us with fear and guilt."

The church is obsessed with sin when it should be obsessed with righteousness. The revelation of sin serves an important role in the lives of those outside of faith, but has no power over those who walk by faith.

Because sin is misunderstood by Christians, it is necessary to explore this topic more fully. We need to understand what the role of sin is, and why it decreases once we are delivered to Christ. Sin must decrease when faith increases. Not understanding these truths becomes a hindrance to faith.

Let's review a few scriptures that help lay the groundwork for understanding sin. We are going to use a lot of scripture in this chapter, and my hope is that once we are done, you'll understand why sin was necessary to point us to Christ, and why sin is irrelevant to those who are in Christ. If that sounds odd to you, I believe you'll be blessed by what we're about to explore.

We have already looked at how Jesus never called a guilty person a sinner, but always confronted the religious elite with their sinful condition. The reason is that the prostitutes and drunkards that gravitated to Jesus knew they were sinners, and they were fully aware of their need for God's gift of righteousness. The religious community had to be shown the worthlessness of human righteousness before they could see their own need. Those who wanted to glorify themselves hated Jesus' message. That's why they persecuted grace. Confronting sin is ONLY for the purpose of showing us the valuelessness of self-righteousness so we can recognize the gift of righteousness through God's love.

With that in mind, let's begin exploring the Bible's teaching on sin and its purpose. First look at the revealer of sin – the law. **Romans 7:13**

> Has then what is good become death to me? Certainly not!
> But sin, that it might appear sin, was producing death in
> me through what is good, so that sin through the
> commandment might become exceedingly sinful.

The law was given, not to show us how to be good, but to show us how sinful we are in our natural state. The problem with human pride is that sin appears to be good. Because we have a flawed perspective, we think we are doing good when we present human self-righteousness as we attempt to feel justified. Therefore, the law was given that instead of appearing to be good, sin might appear to be sin – in other words, the law unmasks sin to reveal it as sin so we can see it.

Not only that, but as the law unveils sin in all its forms, it makes us exceedingly sinful. For this reason, the Apostle Paul asks a natural question, "Has what is good (the law) become death?" Sin produces death, so doesn't the law that unveils sin equal death also? Is the law bad? Certainly not. The commandments of the law are designed to strip away every masquerade of false righteousness so each person can recognize that nothing good comes from man. The Bible then explains why this is important in **Romans 5:20-21**

^{20} Moreover the law entered that the offense might abound. But where sin abounded, grace abounded much more,

^{21} so that as sin reigned in death, even so grace might reign through righteousness to eternal life through Jesus Christ our Lord.

The law makes sin abound by unveiling it in all its forms so that God's gift of grace may also be revealed for what it is, the unearned and unearnable gift of God's righteousness. Until we can recognize that sin is founded upon death, condemning us to die with it, we can't know to look outside of ourselves where we can see the gift of righteousness, which is founded upon eternal life. The Bible reaffirms this truth in **Romans 3:20-21**

^{20} Therefore by the deeds of the law no flesh will be justified in His sight, for by the law *is* the knowledge of sin.

^{21} But now the righteousness of God apart from the law is revealed, being witnessed by the Law and the Prophets,

Once again, we are taught that the law is NOT a merit system. It is a conviction system. Its purpose is to give us the knowledge of sin so we can trust in God's righteousness, which delivers us from sin. We have got to understand that we are righteous for one reason and one reason only – God has given us His righteousness as a gift without merit, and we can only receive it by faith.

The law produces the knowledge of sin, makes us guilty before God, nullifies all human attempts at righteousness, and does this so it can lead us to Christ. The law is our tutor – the one charged with preparing us for our adoption as children of God. Take to heart the words of **Galatians 3:24-25**

^{24} Therefore the law was our tutor *to bring us* to Christ, that we might be justified by faith.

^{25} But after faith has come, we are no longer under a tutor.

Not only does the law unveil our need by exposing our sin so we are prepared to receive Christ, but once we've been delivered to Christ, there is no longer a need for our tutor. The law has served its purpose by revealing to us that all mankind can produce is sin, it relinquishes its role and is discharged from its duty of condemnation. Condemnation becomes irrelevant to the person who has been justified by faith. Once we are in faith, the law has no purpose and sin has no power.

This is the only message of sin the church should be preaching. Once we are in Christ, we are not under that tutelage. Why are we pointing people back to the law when the Bible clearly says it has come to an end to those who are of faith? Let's be reminded of the words of **Romans 10:4**

For Christ *is* the end of the law for righteousness to everyone who believes.

Add to this **Galatians 5:18**
But if you are led by the Spirit, you are not under the law.

It's time to stop preaching condemnation by law to those whom the Bible has declared are not and cannot be under condemnation because they are in Christ.

People don't believe Christ has the power to transform us without law. This is because they are trying to interpret the words of spirit and life through a mind drawing from the flesh. If you tell the fleshly mind there are no rules, it naturally thinks of ways it can indulge itself in the flesh. If you tell the spiritually minded there is no law, it rejoices in the freedom to leave behind the weak and beggarly things of the flesh so it can pursue life.[27]

People only trust in the law for two reasons. They don't believe the Spirit has the power to transform us from a sinful nature to a godly one, but they believe man does have the power of becoming good by self-effort. It's a combination of disbelief in God, and the pride of man. As long as our proud heart believes we can make ourselves good, we won't let go of our hope of

---

[27] Galatians 4:9

meriting our own righteousness through the law. The Apostle Paul gives us a great insight into the impossibility of this.

Paul is the pinnacle of spiritual maturity. He received direct revelation from God that was so powerful, God gave him a thorn in the flesh to keep him humble and in the state of mind that understood complete dependence upon God. The Lord used Paul to write two-thirds of the New Testament, and when his enemies stoned him and left him for dead, God used this event to give even greater revelation. He was caught up into the third heaven. He later testified that he saw and heard things that is unlawful for men to speak.[28]

Who has witnessed deeper things of the Spirit than what Paul experienced? Yet he looked at himself and said, "In me, that is in my flesh, nothing good dwells." Nothing good dwells? Not good works, righteousness, or godliness. In fact, Paul explained that our flesh can do nothing but serve the law of sin. He looked at himself and acknowledged the same struggles you and I have. Look at **Romans 7:17-21**

17 But now, *it is* no longer I who do it, but sin that dwells in me.

18 For I know that in me (that is, in my flesh) nothing good dwells; for to will is present with me, but *how* to perform what is good I do not find.

19 For the good that I will *to do*, I do not do; but the evil I will not *to do*, that I practice.

20 Now if I do what I will not *to do*, it is no longer I who do it, but sin that dwells in me.

21 I find then a law, that evil is present with me, the one who wills to do good.

In these passages we find a critical truth that legalistic (or righteousness by self-effort) thinking can't comprehend. When you look to yourself, instead of finding righteousness, you will discover that evil is present with you. Yes, though you desire to do good, like Paul, you will find that even though you try to do what is good, sin still has dominion over your flesh. It either

---

[28] 2 Corinthians 12:2-4

causes you to do what is sinful, or it hijacks your attempt at righteousness. The flesh uses any resource we permit it to have to glorify the flesh and become puffed up with pride and self-glorification.

Take special note of his acknowledgement that sin is always present with him in the flesh, yet he also says that when he sins, it is not he that sins, but it is sin that remains in his members (body of flesh) that does the evil. This agrees with **1 John 3:9**

> Whoever has been born of God does not sin, for His seed remains in him; and he cannot sin, because he has been born of God.

You are not your body of flesh. If you have been born again through faith in Christ, you are a spiritual creation that is born of God, abides in God, and is a partaker of God. If you attempt to live the Christian life through the flesh, you will find that evil is present with you, and it thwarts the good you desire to do. You cannot serve God in the flesh. That means you cannot serve or obey God through human effort. The mind set on yourself will never please God and will struggle to have a consistent walk of faith. It certainly can never produce spiritual maturity. Look at how Paul explains this beautifully in **Romans 7:22-23**

> 22 For I delight in the law of God according to the inward man.
>
> 23 But I see another law in my members, warring against the law of my mind, and bringing me into captivity to the law of sin which is in my members.

Your inner man, the spiritual life that has been born of God and born within you through Christ, that nature delights in the law of God. You don't have to force yourself to do good. Your new man grieves over sin and craves righteousness.

Though this is true, the law of sin still works in your body of flesh, craving sin. Your flesh desires the life of sin that your old nature once delighted in. Therefore, it wars against your mind trying to draw you back in the flesh where you can do nothing but serve sin.

This is true whether you are pursuing lusts or trying to produce righteousness without God. The one who tries to become righteous for God is actually setting their minds back in the flesh and is serving the flesh and not God. Paul concludes this explanation of our inner struggle with **Romans 7:25**

I thank God-- through Jesus Christ our Lord! So then, with the mind I myself serve the law of God, but with the flesh the law of sin.

Don't lose sight of this vital truth. If you try to serve God in the flesh, it is impossible. The flesh ONLY serves the law of sin. The mind in the Spirit ONLY serves the law of God. Also keep in mind that the very next verse gives us the assurance that there is now no condemnation to us who are in Christ, and have our life in the Spirit. (See Romans 8:1 and 8:9)

If your mind is in the Spirit, you cannot sin, the law has no jurisdiction, and you will do by nature the things that are of God. What the flesh could not do, you will naturally do without the law. So there are only two options. We can try to keep the law (which God will not empower us to do) and let the flesh try to become righteous for God, or we can trust in Christ and live according to our inner man, which is already in agreement with the law – even if we have no clue what that law is.

God will never empower you to do what Christ has already done. God does not want you to overcome sin, He wants you to trust in Christ who has already overcome sin for you.

When Jesus sent His disciples to sail to the other side of the Sea of Galilee, it was the call of the law versus grace. In the Old Testament, God gave the law and told the people to go to the other side of the desert and enter the Promised Land. They could not accomplish this work because man is the weakness of the law. Those who trusted in themselves buckled when human faith was tested. When man failed to stand by faith, God declared, "You will never enter my rest." No promise can be received outside of faith. God then gave them the law knowing man could not do what was commanded. The purpose of the command was to reveal to man that what was impossible with man was not only possible with God, but was also God's gift that supplied what man lacked.

As we studied earlier, man under the law could not enter the promise, but when God's people followed Joshua (a picture of Christ), the promise was entered without effort or hindrance. Even the raging waters lost their power when mankind walked by faith.

God gave us another word-picture of this when Jesus told His disciples to go to the other side of the Sea of Galilee. It was a command Jesus knew they could not accomplish. Yet, they gave it their best effort. Just as the disciples thought they were making progress, a mighty storm arose and blew against the boat, driving them backward away from their goal. Jesus stood on a mountain and watched them rowing fruitlessly against the wind. He waited until they reached the point of exhaustion, and then He came to them walking on the water.

The wind and the waves had no power over Jesus, and as He approached the boat the men cried out in fear. Jesus comforted them and said, "It is I. Do not be afraid." Peter asked to join Christ and Jesus said, "Come." It's the same call you and I have. We are called to not be afraid of sin, the world, or even our own weaknesses. The invitation from Him is to come and join Him where the winds have no power.

Peter stepped onto the waters and walked toward Christ. For a few precious steps, Peter did what was humanly impossible. The wind had no power. The water became a firm foundation under his feet. No doubt every disciple stood in astonishment at this act of walking in the Spirit by faith. As he beheld Christ, Peter was being transformed into that same glory.

Then the tempter came. The accuser said, "Look at the wind blowing your hair into your eyes. Isn't this the same wind that twelve of you couldn't row against? You certainly can't stand. Look at the waves. These are the waves that nearly sank the ship. When one hits you, you are doomed."

Peter took his eyes off Jesus and tried to brace himself for the wave. In that instant, the foundation of his feet failed and he fell into the sea. He would have certainly drowned if not for the mercy of Christ to pluck him back out. Jesus' words to Peter are the same to you and me. "O you of little faith. Why did you doubt?"

The church is still listening to the accuser who says, "You can't walk above sin. Look at how it defeated you before Christ. Get back in the boat of religion where you are safe. Trust in the rules and submit back under them. You can't walk on the water."

Of course you can't walk on the water. Of course you can't overcome sin. Of course the death of the law can't overcome sin. But here's a secret. It's not about you. It's about Christ and His power to overcome, AND His invitation for you to join Him in the Spirit where sin, the flesh, and the law have no power.

Are we so faithless that we've taken a few precious steps onto the water by faith when we received life by answering Jesus' call to come, but now we doubt what we have already experienced, but have taken our eyes off Christ to look at the waves of sin and the flesh? We then return our trust to the power of sin, thus giving it the ability to defeat us

Here is a great truth you must understand in order to experience the true life in the Spirit. Sin only has power over the flesh. Sin cannot knock you off your feet unless you take your eyes off Christ. Temptation calls for us to turn from Christ to pursue the empty promise of satisfaction without God. God promised, "To those who trust under the shadow of My wings, I will give them to drink from the rivers of My pleasures."[29] God promised that under His blessing, we are rich and He adds no sorrows with it.[30] The world cannot make that promise.

We are also distracted by religion. When I take my eyes off Christ to do something that is dependent upon what I do, instead of what He has done, I have submitted myself back to the waves. When I hear the call from the pulpit, "Look at your sin," it is a call to take my eyes off Jesus and look to myself. Then I cannot stand.

When I fail or see inadequacies in myself or others. I am looking to something other than Christ, and I cannot stand. In myself, I will always see inadequacy. I will fall short, and if I

---

[29] Psalm 36:7-8
[30] Proverbs 10:22

believe my acceptance with God is conditional upon my performance, I cannot stand. If I look down at others, or reject my brothers and sisters in Christ because they are incapable of being perfect or measuring up to my expectations, I have placed my dependency and expectation on someone other than Christ, and cannot stand in the life of the Spirit.

When I blow it, I am not called to grovel in failure or guilt. I am called to live according to **2 Corinthians 3:18**

But we all, with unveiled face, beholding as in a mirror the glory of the Lord, are being transformed into the same image from glory to glory, just as by the Spirit of the Lord.

We've viewed this passage many times and should view it many more. Our unveiled face has had all distractions removed. We are beholding only the glory of Christ, and as we do so, we have the promise that the Spirit of God will transform us into that same image. Success is not dependent upon you. It's the work of God for the glory of His grace. Every distraction is the enemy's attempt to get you to look at anything other than Christ.

We are often distracted from the power of the Spirit, and this is true whether we are pursuing what we think is sin, or what we think is righteous. Anything that is not from Christ is of the flesh and is sin, but in the Spirit, the things of the world (including the flesh) have no power.

You have been invited to walk on the water with Christ!

Discussion Questions

Is the law a merit system?

Can a sinner become good through keeping the law?

How does revealing sin also reveal grace?

What does the Bible mean when it says the law was our tutor, but after faith has come, we are no longer under a tutor?

What does the Bible mean by, "If you are led by the Spirit, you are not under the law?"

How can a Christian be a new creation, but still have sin always present with them?

Review Romans 7:25. Is it possible to try to serve God but actually be serving sin?

How do we not serve sin?

Why did Jesus invite Peter on the water?

How does Peter's failure, even though he experienced God's power in his life, mirror our struggles and lack of faith?

Explain why we fail to walk on the water in our Christian lives.

Explain what 2 Corinthians 3:18 means in your Christian life.

Why Sin is Not Imputed

After looking at the defeat of sin, let's ask the one burning question that causes people to resist the message of complete trust in Christ. What happens when we sin? Do we confess sin?

No. We confess Christ. We confess our Advocate. There is only one place in the new covenant of Christ where anyone is told to confess sin, and we'll explain what is being taught there shortly. The act of confessing sin was and is an acknowledgement that someone is unredeemed and not under the payment of sin, Jesus Christ. The Old Testament sacrificial system was intended to force people to look at their sin and their guilt under the law. Jesus presented sin to all who trusted in their own righteousness, but declared to the sinner, "Neither do I condemn you."

Before we examine the call to the unredeemed to confess their sins, let's review the double-blessing given to us who are in Christ. **Romans 4:7-8**

7 "Blessed *are those* whose lawless deeds are forgiven,
And whose sins are covered;
8 Blessed *is the* man to whom the LORD shall not impute sin."

If God will not impute sin, what is the purpose of proclaiming to God what He has refused to impute to you? Are you blessed? Do you believe this promise? According to this passage and the rest of Romans 4, those who enter the promise by faith have this double-blessing. Actually, it's a triple blessing, for the one who believes God has the following blessing as well. **Romans 4:22-25**

22 And therefore "it was accounted to him for righteousness."
23 Now it was not written for his sake alone that it was imputed to him,
24 but also for us. It shall be imputed to us who believe in Him who raised up Jesus our Lord from the dead,

[25] who was delivered up because of our offenses, and was raised because of our justification.

Let's consider the triple-blessing. God imputes His righteousness to us. We cannot earn righteousness or accomplish righteousness. God imputes (or credits to our account) His own righteousness. That means when God looks at you, His child, He says, "You are the righteousness of God in Christ."[31] There is no higher righteousness. Any other righteousness would be a step down and a counterfeit, so there is nothing else to obtain.

The second part of the blessing is, blessed is the one whose lawless deeds are forgiven, and whose sins are covered. This applies to all our past sins while we were under the law. God took all the written account against us that stood as our accuser, and He took it out of the way by nailing it to the cross.[32] Not only that, but the written account of the law that stood contrary to us was also nailed to the cross (See Colossians 2:14).

This leads right in to the third part of our blessing. "Blessed is the one whom the Lord shall not impute sin." Stop and meditate on this for a moment. God imputes us with His righteousness, but will not impute our own sins to us. This refers to our own sins, not the sins of others. So this is sins we commit, but are not imputed – or credited – against us. This can only refer to our future sins.

Our past sins were forgiven and covered, and our future sins cannot be imputed to us. Hard to believe? By human reasoning, it is. Is that a license to sin? Not exactly. It does give us the freedom to choose whether to live according to the flesh or walk with God in the Spirit. It also gives us true freedom knowing that when we blow it, wrath does not come back upon us, and we do not need to stay in the flesh by focusing on our sins and failures.

Instead of remaining in the flesh, we can immediately come boldly before God's throne of grace to find help in our time of

---

[31] 2 Corinthians 5:21
[32] Colossians 2:13-14

need – the time when our flesh has warred against our mind and gotten a temporary victory. It is like Peter, when he was distracted from Christ, he fell into the flesh and cried out for grace. Jesus plucked him out so the world could not swallow him up.

That is what God wants from you. Don't stay in defeat. Cry out for the power of grace and God will lift you up. And He won't make you recount all your sins to do it. Jesus didn't blast Peter for falling. His only question was, "Why did you doubt?" When you fall into the flesh, it's for the same reason. You doubt God's provision, protection, or promises. So you take your eyes off Christ and look to the stormy world around you.

Remember what we read in a previous chapter? Romans 5:13 explains that even though sin is in the world, sin is not imputed where there is no law. Sin still harms the one who submits to it, but God does not withdraw His promises when we sin. In fact, He reaches out through grace to pluck us out of the flesh again. But if we don't believe God's promise not to impute sin, we'll turn away from Him in shame instead of toward Him in faith.

If we lost God's grace when we sinned, the new covenant would be no better than the old. If we fell back under condemnation when we sinned, the work of Christ would have no more power to change us than the law did. If the work of sin could break our fellowship with God, then our works of the flesh would be more powerful than the work of Christ. Can sin defeat grace? Can the works of our flesh defeat Christ? If anything you do can undo what Jesus has accomplished, our faith is in vain.

Thankfully, this is not the case. According to the Bible, those who are in the Spirit (who are those born into Christ) are no longer under the law. According to the Bible, we have (past tense) fulfilled the law because we are in Christ. According to the Bible, Jesus is the end of the law of righteousness for everyone who believes. According to the Bible, the law of the Spirit of life has set us free from the law of sin and death.

Both the law of righteousness (what we must do) and the law of sin and death (the consequences of what we have done) have come to an end in Christ. You cannot undo the work of

Christ. Your sin cannot defeat the righteousness of God given to you. Add to this, the Bible says that the gifts and calling of God are irrevocable.[33] God has bound Himself by His word. Because of His promise, God cannot and will not withdraw His gift of righteousness from you. Nor can He or will He withdraw grace or eternal life from you.

God has put no conditions of forgiveness on you other than faith in Christ. Once you entered into Christ, that bond becomes unbreakable. Or as the Bible says, "If we are faithless, He remains faithful, for He cannot deny Himself."[34] That means even if you don't believe in the power of God's promises, it does not change the reality of them. It only changes your ability to see and experience them.

Having said this, let's look at the only New Covenant passage that mentions confessing sin. Look at **1 John 1:9**

If we confess our sins, He is faithful and just to forgive us *our* sins and to cleanse us from all unrighteousness.

So are we to confess sin? If you are an unbeliever, yes. That's the call to acknowledge what we as Christians already know. We cannot be good and nothing good within us dwells. That's why the next verse warns that anyone who thinks he is without sin is calling Christ a liar. Before we dig into the above passage, let's bring in **1 John 2:1**

My little children, these things I write to you, so that you may not sin. And if anyone sins, we have an Advocate with the Father, Jesus Christ the righteous.

Now this is an interesting contrast. The first chapter says to confess we are sinners, and the second chapter tells us that if we sin we are to trust in our Advocate. Is this a contradiction? No. The phrase, "My little children," clues us into a change of audience.

1 John uses something called empathetic reasoning. It's like a teacher mentoring a student who is doing something

---

[33] Romans 11:29
[34] 2 Timothy 2:13

wrong. If a teacher said, "We shouldn't call other people names," is the teacher confessing his own sin of name-calling? No, it's a way to point out a fault without alienating someone. It sounds better than saying, "You are wrong for calling people names." It's the idea of empathizing with someone as you try to persuade them to accept what you are teaching them.

1 John 1 begins with an immediate defense of the gospel. He starts with, "We have seen with our own eyes, we have heard with our own ears, we have touched with our very hands the Word of Life." John then rebuts every belief of the first-century gnostic belief system.

Some have taught that Gnosticism didn't exist in the era of John, but this is an uninformed statement. Gnosticism can be traced as far back as the Persian Empire. Just as it is in Greek Mythology, Gnosticism picks out ideas from other belief systems, and evolves as it incorporates new ideas into its core philosophy. Modern day Gnostics have certain beliefs that were adopted from our culture and New Age beliefs that were prevalent back in the first century.

In the first century (when the epistle of John was written), Gnostics believed in a form of Jesus, but didn't believe he was a physical being. They believed all physical manifestations were evil, and that Jesus was only a spirit and did not come in the flesh. They believed they made themselves sinless through gaining gnosis, or secret knowledge.

John rebuts the gnostic Jesus by explaining that Christ came bodily, and they were eyewitnesses to this fact. He then rebukes the Christianized form of Gnosticism in the first chapter. He also gives us another strong clue to his audience.

In verse 3, John says he declares the things he and the disciples have seen and heard, "That you may have fellowship with us," indicating that he is addressing people who were not yet in the fellowship of the believers.

When chapter 2 begins, John shifts his focus by doing something he did not do in chapter one. Chapter one had no greeting, because he was writing to those who may have come into the church congregation, but were not part of the fellowship of Christ. In 2:1 he greets the church as "My little children," and

Why Sin is Not Imputed

then approaches sin in a completely different way than when he presented it to the Gnostics.

To the unbeliever, the message is, "No one can say they have no sin, and anyone who believes they are sinless is denying Christ. Confess your sins and trust in Christ, who is faithful and just to forgive, and cleanse us from all sin through His blood."

To the church, he is declaring, "I write that you may not sin, but if anyone sins, we have an Advocate, Jesus Christ the righteous." As discussed before, an advocate is a legal defender who pleads the innocence of his client. When Jesus pleads your innocence, there is not anyone in heaven or earth that can condemn you. Many people deny His power, but it doesn't change the fact that if Jesus says you are innocent, you are innocent. And this is written as our assurance when we DO sin.

As stated earlier, God does not want you to overcome your own sin. He is calling you to trust in both His victory over sin and His power to transform you into His likeness. Let's look at a few passages that help clarify this. Look first at the words of Jesus in **John 16:33**

"These things I have spoken to you, that in Me you may have peace. In the world you will have tribulation; but be of good cheer, I have overcome the world."

The flesh is bound to the world as we await our final redemption, where God promised to change our bodies into one like Christ's.[35] Everything of this world is bound to corruption. This is true for our bodies of flesh, and the world system we have to interact with. We will have struggles and tribulation – including the temptations of sin. But our confidence is in Christ, who has overcome the world and has made us into overcomers. When trouble plagues us, we are to be of good cheer because of what He has done, not to focus on what we cannot do. This is explained further in **1 John 5:4**

For whatever is born of God overcomes the world. And this is the victory that has overcome the world-- our faith.

---

[35] 1 Corinthians 15:51-52

Are you born of God? If you are trusting in Christ, you are. And what gives us victory? Resisting sin? Forcing ourselves into the law? Beating ourselves up when we fail? No, there is only one victory – faith in Christ. If you trust in Christ and receive His works, which God credits to you as a free gift of His grace, you ARE and overcomer. Maturity comes as we learn to walk according to who we are in the Spirit so we can decrease our focus on the flesh.

I've never met a victorious Christian who didn't understand the amazing call of grace. I've never met anyone who confessed their way out of the sinful fleshly mindset. I've never met a victorious Christian who walked around saying, "I am a sinner."

You and I are not what our body of flesh craves. According to the Bible, your new life in Christ was created incorruptible, and that which is born of God cannot sin, because it is born of God (who also cannot sin). When you start believing you are who God has declared you to be, learn how to focus on Christ, and learn to walk by faith in the Spirit, the flesh will begin losing its power and you will discover the truth of the above passage, "This is the victory that overcomes the world, your faith."

That is your faith in Christ, what He has done, and the promise that you are triple-blessed. And none of this has anything to do with what you have done right, nor is it about not doing wrong. It's all about what Christ accomplished and offers to you as a free gift.

Let's end by reflecting on a scripture from an earlier passage. Hebrews 10 explains the insufficient sacrifices of the Old Testament by comparing them to what they foreshadowed, Christ. The Bible compares the earthly ordinances with the completed work of Christ, and says that if those sacrifices had been sufficient, there would have been no more consciousness of sin. The Bible then points the people who had been under that system to Christ as their sufficiency.

If the evidence that the old system was insufficient was that they still were conscious of their sins, then the evidence of Christ's sufficiency is that we lose our consciousness of sin.

Why Sin is Not Imputed

This can only happen one way – that our faith is in Christ. Everything in the flesh is sin, for nothing good dwells within me, that is in my flesh. The same is true for you and every other person. Sin indeed causes our flesh to focus on the things that are opposed to the Spirit, but we are no longer of the flesh. When the flesh arises, our victory is to take our eyes off sin and put it on Christ.

This is true whether our eyes are on the false promises of pleasure, the false righteousness of human effort, or if our focus is on the sins we have just committed. The flesh should never be our focus. If it remains our focus, we will be conscious of sin, but if our focus is on Christ, He becomes our sufficiency and sin becomes irrelevant.

There is nothing wrong with being sorry when you sin. There is something wrong with begging God to do what He has already done. Confession then becomes a declaration of unbelief in what God has declared. True repentance is to change the mind from the flesh to the Spirit. False repentance is to confess sin, beg God for forgiveness, and disbelieve in what He has already declared.

You will grieve when you step out of the Spirit to sin. You'll kick yourself, but God will never kick you. The short track to recovery is to regain your focus on Christ, confess His promises, and boldly come to the throne of grace for help – knowing you are already forgiven. Your sins are already covered. You are not trying to re-obtain forgiveness, but are seeking help in your weakness. Help that God delights in giving.

Victory cannot be found in glorifying sin in any of its forms. Confessing sin is giving it victory over Christ. When we believe sin nullifies the promise, we are glorifying sin. When we think we must confess sin, we are giving it power.

You cannot confess enough sin to earn forgiveness. Only a fraction of your sins will even make it to your consciousness. You are completely unaware of most sins you commit, but the Bible says that anything that is not of faith is sin. That means anything you do, don't do, eat, drink, think, or any other action that is not born out of a heart receiving from God's grace is sin. If you are declaring your sins to God, is that an act of faith? Are you glorifying the grace of God? If not, it is sin. Even your confession of sin is sin when you are denying God's promise that sin cannot be imputed again to you.

Stop trying to do the impossible. Since the vast majority of our sin is outside of our consciousness, relinquish the other fraction of sin to the grave where it is also out of our consciousness. This will not cause you to sin. It will cause you to stop focusing on self, where nothing good dwells, and start focusing on Christ, where all good things are imputed to us as gifts of grace.

You can't stop the flesh from sinning. All you can do is learn how to walk in the spirit where the flesh has no power. Let the flesh become what God has declared – irrelevant. There is nothing wrong with being sorry when you sin, but don't stay there. Don't deny God's success because you failed. Step out of failure and into faith. Here is the biblical way of confessing – **Hebrews 10:23**

Let us hold fast the confession of *our* hope without wavering, for He who promised *is* faithful.

Without wavering, hold to your confession of hope in Christ. His promises are unbreakable. It's not about your abilities, but God's promises. Your faith is dependent upon His promise, not your performance. It's all about the praise of His grace. He is faithful, not because you do enough right, but because He has given you a promise that is founded upon Christ and not you.

You will never fix the flesh. You can only walk by faith where sin has no power. Sin tries to bully you with its wind and waves, but Jesus stands upon the waters with only an invitation, "Come." God is pleased by one thing, your faith in His promises and the power to fulfill them. The flesh can be under your feet, but only when your eyes are on Christ!

Why Sin is Not Imputed

Discussion Questions

What three ways does God declare our blessing in Romans 4?

What does the Bible mean when it says that God will not impute sin?

Why is sin no longer imputed?

Why does God impute His righteousness to us?

Can your sins undo the work of Christ?

Why does 1 John 1:9 and 1 John 2:1 approach sin differently?

Explain what Jesus being your advocate means.

According to 1 John 5:4, how does a Christian become victorious?

What is our part in this victory?

According to Hebrews 10:1-2, why did the Old Testament worshippers remain conscious of their sins?

Does Jesus' sacrifice have the same limitations?

Should we be conscious of sin?

According to Hebrews 10:23, what is our confession?

Do you still believe the Christian should confess their sins?

List a reason for your answers and compare them to the scriptures. Are your reasons testimonies of faith in what God has declared?

Do you think understanding that Jesus defeated sin and it can no longer be imputed will cause people to sin more?

The Bible's Threefold Teaching on Sin

Before we leave the topic of sin, I want to address the claim that grace teaching either winks at sin, or denies that sin exists. In the life of the Spirit, sin does not exist, and as we've already discussed, it was defeated on the cross and taken out of the way. Even so, sin is still bound to our flesh where it tries to bring our minds back under its service, but this is only possible when we are not walking by faith.

The idea that grace believers teach that sin is okay or no longer matters is false. In fact, it is legalism that minimizes sin. Legalism only acknowledges 'big sins' or blatant acts of sin, but has no concept of the ever-present sin in the flesh. Legalism doesn't grasp the reality that whatever is not of faith is sin; therefore, any action that is not trusting and receiving from Christ alone is an act of the flesh and is sin.

Legalism also does not acknowledge that Jesus has rendered sin powerless, and that we have escaped the lusts of the flesh through Him. [36] When we don't believe that Christ has defeated sin, we will reject faith and try to use our sinful flesh to defeat the sin in our flesh, which is impossible.

Only grace unmuddies the waters by revealing that the discussion isn't actually about sin or religion, but are we walking by faith in the Spirit, or are we walking in the flesh. There is not a third option, and legalism is always an act of the flesh. It may look good to human eyes, but if we are trusting in our works or our own righteousness, we are in the flesh.

When someone doesn't understand the work of God, they fear it. Nearly every objection against grace teaching is based on the fear of Christians sinning. The reason for this fear is because most simply do not understand the Bible's teaching on sin.

It's easy to get lost in the details, unless we take a step back and study the big-picture view. Let me give a word-picture to explain. There was a young man I worked with who was raised in New York City. He came to Atlanta and we travelled to an

---

[36] 2 Peter 1:4

office where we were going to do some work. Having always been in the city, he thought the whole world was covered with pavement.

In a conversation, he said, "If we don't do something, the world is going to run out of trees. There are only a few left!"

There was no convincing him otherwise. He had seen it his whole life. Trees plowed down, and buildings, roads, and parking lots took their place. We had to fly from the east coast to the west coast. I asked him to try for a window seat, and then look out the window at the landscape below during our four to five hour flight.

Having flown before, I knew what he would see. When you are surrounded by city buildings, it looks like the whole world is nothing but buildings, but when you are flying at 30,000 feet, it gives you a new perspective. For the first five minutes of flying time, there was nothing but city below, but when we left the city, we saw nothing but trees.

During our two-thousand mile flight, he discovered something he never knew. There was a dot for a city, and then hundreds of miles of forest land. Then a brief view of a city and miles of forest again.

The truth that I could never convince my coworker to believe was understood once he had a big-picture view. The same is true when we study the scriptures. People get entrenched in pet doctrines that blind them to the reality of God's purpose, and arguing against misconceptions rarely works. But if we can persuade someone to take a big-picture view, then the details that once seemed to be the entire biblical view are shown in their true meaning. But without a Bible-wide perspective, it is easy to draw misconceptions by bogging down into one detail, and treating it as though it is the whole meaning of God's word.

Until someone gains the big picture view, doctrine remains 'my belief system' versus 'your belief system'. When people argue over doctrine, it's like someone in Arizona trying to convince someone in Georgia that the world is a desert, and the person in Georgia trying to convince someone in the flatlands of Nebraska that if they don't see mountains, they are just blind.

Threefold Teaching on Sin

Each side is misapplying a fact in an attempt to negate someone else's fact. There are indeed false teachings, but rarely is there a denomination that does not have misguided teaching. The more you learn to study both the details and the big picture of the word, the more you'll discovered that your previous understanding was flawed, because although you may have had some facts correct, your assumptions were wrong because you didn't see how they fit with the rest of scripture.

I say all of this as a prelude to our discussion about sin. The reason grace opponents fear what they call hyper-grace is because they are viewing it as though it's opposing what they have always been taught. The reason people believe grace teaching justifies a sinful lifestyle is because they are bogged down in the details of one perspective of sin, and have little or no concept of the Bible's teaching of sin.

The truth is the Bible gives us three teachings on sin, each serving a purpose that either drives us to Christ, sets us free from fear, or directs us away from the false promises of the flesh. False promises of religious flesh are just as much a part of sin as lustful flesh. Take to heart the words of **2 Timothy 2:15**

> Be diligent to present yourself approved to God, a worker who does not need to be ashamed, rightly dividing the word of truth.

Some translations use the word 'study' instead of diligent, but the Greek word 'spoudazo' means to give diligence or exert one's self to an endeavor. Of course, our diligence is found in study, prayer, and meditation on the word. Study alone will not give understanding. There must be revelation through the Spirit. God promised to give understanding and wisdom to those who receive the word, and diligently seek understanding from Him.[37] The Bible explains that it is the Holy Spirit who anoints us with that understanding, not our intellect.[38]

We must be diligent in our seeking of God's revelation as we study the word, so we can 'rightly divide' the word of truth.

---

[37] Proverbs 2:1-9
[38] 1 John 2:27

You can wrongly divide. You can also stay at a distance and never divide it at all. The learning disciple will prayerfully study as they learn to see the bigger picture, and then they will dig out important truths by dividing it from the whole to examine and discover deeper insights. Look at the promise of **Proverbs 2:3-7**

> ³ Yes, if you cry out for discernment, *And* lift up your voice for understanding,
> ⁴ If you seek her as silver, And search for her as *for* hidden treasures;
> ⁵ Then you will understand the fear of the LORD, And find the knowledge of God.
> ⁶ For the LORD gives wisdom; From His mouth *come* knowledge and understanding;
> ⁷ He stores up sound wisdom for the upright; *He is* a shield to those who walk uprightly;

The treasures of God are waiting for you to discover them. A book like this may inspire or encourage you, but nothing compares to discovering what God has stored up for you to find. And it doesn't come from just reading. Nor does it come from mere study. It comes from God's revelation, and is a guarantee to those who diligently seek it. To diligently seek is to seek until you find.

There have been scriptures that troubled me because I knew I was missing something. I had the knowledge, but not the understanding. I've dedicated weeks of study to understand passages where I knew I lacked revelation. God doesn't always reveal understanding immediately. Sometimes He calls us to diligently seek, and only reveals to us when we have sought, pursued with our whole heart, and hungered for the truth. God never promises to give understanding to the flippant reader of the word, who expects God to reward them, because they paid their dues with their daily reading.

The more we hunger for the word and cry out for understanding, the more we are abandoning our own abilities and the human intellect so we can be drawn into the Spirit, where God awaits with the treasures of the words of life.

This is very much true for the church's favorite topic – sin. God does not want us to be obsessed with sin – ours or the world's. He wants us to understand the work of Christ and sin is a powerful way of unveiling Christ. Unfortunately, the church is stuck at the front-side of the cross where sin is exposed, but never goes beyond this. Consider the command of **Hebrews 6:1**

> Therefore, leaving the discussion of the elementary *principles* of Christ, let us go on to perfection, not laying again the foundation of repentance from dead works and of faith toward God,

God does not want you to be stuck in perpetual repentance. The Lord's desire is for you to grow out of immaturity, but most Christians are stuck laying and re-laying the foundation of repentance from sin again and again, but never go on toward perfection. And that is what we are about to discover with the Bible's threefold teaching on sin.

Repentance

The first doctrine of sin in the Bible is the call for repentance. Repentance from sin plays an important role in our faith. It is the point to where a sinner fully understands that they are a sinful creature, and cannot make themselves righteous. Contrary to what most people think, repent does not mean to be sorry for your sins, though sorrow over sin does drive people to repentance.

The word 'repent' comes from the Greek word 'metanoeo' which means to change one's mind. For the unredeemed soul, it is to change the mind from trying to earn our own righteousness to recognizing one cannot become righteous. Therefore the mind is turned to Christ.

For the redeemed Christian, to repent means to change our mind from a fleshly way of thinking to a spiritual way of thinking. It is to recognize we have allowed our mind to be controlled by our flesh, and we place our mind back in the Spirit by placing our trust in Christ. We trust in the power of His righteousness given to us, and we trust in the power of the Spirit to overcome our flesh.

The first teaching of sin in the Bible is the revelation of our hopeless condition. As discussed earlier, the law was given to show mankind that he is guilty when he looks to his own righteousness. The fleshly mind cannot understand this without trial and failure. The law demands our righteousness so we can understand we are not righteous, and cannot make ourselves righteous.

The law gives sin its power in us, so we are driven to the cross, where sin is defeated. This is explained in these two passages.

Romans 5:20

Moreover the law entered that the offense might abound. But where sin abounded, grace abounded much more

1 Corinthians 15:56

The sting of death *is* sin, and the strength of sin *is* the law.

God strengthened sin through the law so the flesh could be defeated. Once sin abounds in us and defeats all human righteousness, God reveals grace so we can see that grace abounds over sin and defeats it.

When we are stuck in the details of sin, it's easy to focus on sin, and never realize why God allowed sin to reign in the flesh. In fact, most sin-focused teaching does not acknowledge that God empowered sin. Without a 30,000 foot view, people can be focused on the era of the law and still be fighting to overcome sin, as if man has the power to do so. They do not yet realize sin has been defeated, nor do they realize that the law's purpose was to drive them to Christ, instead of demanding their own righteousness.

Those who don't understand that sin's purpose is to make us guilty, and the law's purpose is to reveal our guilt, they will try to twist the law into a merit system instead of understanding the Bible's teaching that it is a condemnation system.

We teach what sin is, so those outside of Christ can see their condition, for until we see the abounding sin within us, we have a very hard time seeing our need for the abounding grace given through Christ. We preach sin ONLY to make the guilty understand their guilt, so people can stop looking at self-righteousness that they may have eyes to see the gift of righteousness through Christ.

Once someone is in Christ, the guilt and condemnation of sin no longer applies. This message only applies to those outside of Christ. If we continue to preach condemnation to the believer, we have nullified the work of Christ and are denying the glory of God's grace.

The church must rightly divide the word of truth. Sin is preached to those who are under the law, that every mouth may be stopped and the world become guilty before God.[39] This is *so that* the law drives them to Christ, where they are taught to abandon human effort and trust in Christ,[40] who has both taken the penalty of sin, and has fulfilled the law on our behalf.[41]

If the church takes the message God intended for those who are not in Christ, and teaches that message to believers who are already in Christ, we are driving people back into the flesh. So then the message that was intended to reveal to unbelievers the condition of their flesh, is being twisted to convince Christians they are still of the flesh. That is not rightly dividing the word of truth.

Deliverance from Sin and Wrath

The Bible's second teaching on sin is the Christian's victory over it. Let's review the message of the Holiest Place in the temple we discussed previously. In the center of the temple was a veiled area called the Holiest of Holies. It was a place where the mercy seat of God was located, and was reserved for God alone.

Only once a year was the High Priest allowed to enter and make intercession for the sins of the people. Even then, he had

---

[39] Romans 3:19-20
[40] Galatians 3:24-25
[41] Romans 8:3-4, Galatians 5:18

to go through many cleansing rituals and be purified through ordinances we now know pointed to Christ. It was a fearful thing to come into the holiest place of the temple, and there were times when priests died in there.

When sin encounters holiness, it is destroyed. When sin encounters God's righteousness, it is vanquished. It is not God that is harmed by sin. It is the possessor of sin that is destroyed. Nothing unholy can stand before God. To protect the people, a veil was erected around God's holiness. It was a picture that sin was a barrier between us and God. As long as we had sin, we could not come into God's presence without judgment against sin.

But when Jesus paid the penalty of sin, became sin for us, took our flesh and the law that condemned the flesh out of the way by nailing it to the cross, everything changed.

The moment Jesus died, the veil of the temple, the veil that stood as a barrier between mankind and the holiness of God, was torn from top to bottom. It was God's way of declaring that victory was not man reaching up to God, but God reaching down to man. God tore the veil from Heaven's side, exposing the forbidden Holiest of Holies to the entire world.

The place where only the High Priest could visit, and also feared for his life while in there, was now open to all. This is why Hebrews 4:16 commands us to come boldly (or confidently) before the throne of grace. Even the High Priest could not approach boldly under the old covenant, because he was still a possessor of sin. Through rituals he symbolically covered his sin through the coming Christ, but the foreshadow of Christ could never produce the boldness we have now been given.

Do you realize the magnitude of our command / invitation to come before God's throne with confidence? Those under the old covenant had to quake in fear, but we can approach with confidence. The Old Testament saints were commanded to never approach God or they would die. We are commanded to come before God with joyful expectation. This was not possible while sin was present, but once Jesus defeated sin, the throne of God was immediately opened. You and I have what no Old

Testament saint could possess – a welcome mat into the Holiest of Holies.

We won't go into the details of the Bible's teaching that sin has been removed, since we have already discussed this in previous chapters, but we must believe the word of God. We cannot walk in the Spirit without walking by faith, and we can't walk by faith if we still believe in the power of sin.

We are completely accepted by God because sin was removed through Christ. I don't know a single Christian that would say that when we sin, Christ is defeated. Yet this is exactly what we are teaching when we say that sin separates the Christian from God. The Bible NEVER says this. It says just the opposite. We come confidently before the throne of grace when we are in need – which is when sin is defeating us. Let's revisit this promise because it is important that faith comes by hearing the word of God.[42] Meditate on **Hebrews 4:16**

> Let us therefore come boldly to the throne of grace, that we
> may obtain mercy and find grace to help in time of need.

Let each word of this scripture sink into your heart. This promises that the throne of God's unmerited favor is where we find mercy (not getting any punishment we deserve) and grace (the gifts of God we have not earned) to help us when we are in need. Never are we told that we must get our lives right or confess our sins before we can approach God.

To believe such a thing is to go back under the law and make the new covenant no better than the old. Hebrews 10 warns us that if we willfully sin against God by returning to the law, we are insulting the Spirit of Grace and calling the blood of Christ a common thing. It is to put Jesus' completed work on par with man-dependent religion. Just as legalistic religion falls into ruins when we fail, to deny that sin has been defeated in Christ is to put the cross on the same common ground as human-effort based religion.

The Bible teaches that sin cannot defeat us. Sin cannot nullify the work of Christ. Sin cannot take us outside of Christ.

---

[42] Romans 10:17

Yet Christianized religion has stripped the gospel of its power by rejecting the confidence given to us, and exalting sin over Christ. If you are like me, you have been taught to exalt the power of sin over the power of Christ. Yet this is a denial of the faith. Look at this amazing promise of **Romans 5:10**

> For if when we were enemies we were reconciled to God through the death of His Son, much more, having been reconciled, we shall be saved by His life.

Do you grasp the magnitude of what the Bible is saying here? If God reconciled you while you were in sin, and enemy of God, and nothing more than a sinner living for the flesh, how much more does God continue to save you through the life of Christ? If God was able to conquer sin when you were outside of Christ, how much more power over sin is promised to us who are now in Christ?

If God transformed you when you had a sinful nature, this pales in comparison to the life of Christ in you now that you have both a new spirit and the Holy Spirit within you. Sin cannot defeat you. Sin can only bluff you into submission, which is the final topic of sin we'll discuss.

Don't allow people to defeat you with fear. Don't allow Satan to defeat you with condemnation. You are more than a conqueror through Christ.[43] A conqueror is someone who already has the victory, but if you don't believe, you'll live as one who has no faith. Meditate also on **1 John 5:4-5**

> 4 For whatever is born of God overcomes the world. And this is the victory that has overcome the world-- our faith.
> 5 Who is he who overcomes the world, but he who believes that Jesus is the Son of God?

Where is victory found? In confessing sin? In overcoming sin by your best effort? No, you find victory only one way – faith in Christ. When sin tries to defeat you, it is defeated when you account your flesh as dead,[44] and believe you are the

---

[43] Romans 8:37
[44] Romans 6:11

righteousness of Christ, as God has declared.[45] When you trust more in the finished work of Christ than your own weaknesses, you'll discover victory. When you trust more in the throne of grace than you do in the power of sin, you'll find victory.

The truth is, you are already a victor, but that is a gift of God only obtained through faith in Christ. You must believe that Jesus has power over your flesh. You must believe that you are accepted in the Beloved. Until then, you'll cower from God instead of climbing into His lap on the throne of grace, where help is always given, and love is never denied!

---

[45] 2 Corinthians 5:21, Romans 5:17, Romans 4:5

Discussion Questions

Once someone understands the magnitude of sin outside of Christ, how does this affect their attempts at becoming righteous by what they do?

What's the difference between mental comprehension of the Bible and the Spirit's revelation of truth?

Explain the meaning of repentance.

Review 1 Corinthians 15:56. Why did God give sin the strength to defeat us?

Read Romans 8:9-11. Are you of the flesh? Is sin in the Spirit?

Review Numbers 18:22 and Hebrews 4:16. What changed?

Why did God emphasize fear in the Old Testament, but commands us not to have fear in the New Testament?

Can a Christian walk by faith if they still believe in the power of sin? Explain.

Define both mercy and grace. What do these words teach us about God's design for the Christian life?

Can your sin defeat the work of Christ?

Does the average teaching on sin exalt sin and decrease Christ? What about your belief when you struggle with sin? Do you exalt Christ over sin or the other way around?

Review 1 John 5:4-5. Do you need to overcome sin?

What must a Christian do when sin interferes with their life in the Spirit?

Does God ever withdraw from the Christian?

The Boundaries between Faith and the Flesh

The third doctrine of sin taught in the New Testament is the boundaries of sin. Just as a parent establishes boundaries for their children, God does the same with His children. A three-year-old has no comprehension of the dangers of an electrical outlet. Explaining to a toddler the physics of electricity would do no good. A parent puts safety plugs in the outlet and if a child tries to play with it, we say, "No. That's bad. It will hurt you."

A teen doesn't understand the consequences of going to wild parties or participating in all the activities that look fun to their inexperienced eyes, but a parent can see past the perception of youthful ideals. We may have experienced the pain of foolish choices, or had a friend who suffered great loss. We've seen the end result that a teenager has no comprehension of.

At times, it's impossible to reason with them. All they can see is the enjoyment of what looks fun, and may even promise the parent that they are wise enough to dabble on the edge of danger without falling. When leading by influence fails, a parent often has to fall back on a command. You cannot go. You cannot do that. I don't care if everyone else is doing it, as long as you are under my rules, you won't be like everyone else.

For the child of God, we have a loving Heavenly Father who leads us in the right way, but also sets clear boundaries for our good. God's commandments either point us to the way where blessings flow, or restricts us from going the way where consequences flow. We have a limited human perspective, and cannot see how our choices affect our lives in the future, but God does.

There is a critical truth we must understand when looking at God's commands. These are not conditions on our relationship with Him, His love for us, or our gifts of His grace. God's commandments do not make you righteous. You don't become righteous because you obey. No one is accounted as righteous because they don't sin, nor can we nullify the righteousness of God through human choices. God's righteousness is His gift to those who believed, and the Bible says the gifts and calling of God are irrevocable.

God's righteousness is a gift to you. Your righteousness is meaningless in the life of the Spirit. All good must come from God to us, and when you are not good, it does not destroy the righteousness of God. Your sin is not greater than God's righteousness. You are not a god; therefore, you do not have the power to harm anything that emerges from God. To believe your actions make you righteous is self-idolatry. To believe you can destroy God's gift of righteousness by your actions is also self-idolatry.

There are indeed consequences to sin, but we have to understand that sin is in the flesh, righteousness is in the Spirit. It's a one-way flow. The life in the Spirit indeed flows out into the flesh and will affect our outward behavior to make our actions more godly, but it does not work the other way around.

Your outward behavior cannot improve or harm the life of the Spirit. Your flesh has no power over the new spirit you have received from God. It cannot make your spiritual life any better; it cannot make your spiritual life any worse. Your behavior only hinders or receives the life of the Spirit into your outer man. The mind in the flesh will prevent you from experiencing the new life God has placed within you, but it cannot destroy your new spirit, which is born of God. Consider **Colossians 3:2-3**

2 Set your mind on things above, not on things on the earth.

3 For you died, and your life is hidden with Christ in God.

Your old sinful life died and was taken out of the way. Your new life is hidden with Christ in God! If your life is hidden in God, do you think sin can storm the gates of heaven, overcome God, and destroy the life He is protecting and nurturing? Any who believe that our spiritual life is fragile and vulnerable to the power of sin has little faith in the power of God.

This is where most Christians fail. People live in rollercoaster Christianity because they are trying to use the flesh to feed and protect their spirit. The average Christian believes that sin overthrows the power of God within them, so they turn to themselves and begin trusting in human effort. They also try to become more godly by what they do or don't do. Most people think, if I can just bring this sin under control, I can be more godly and become a better Christian. But God has designed the Christian life from the top down, not the bottom up.

If you look at God's commands as "If I do, I will become," or "If I don't sin, I will become more spiritual," you are trying to swim upstream against a raging current. The best you can hope for is to do better than the people around you, but you will never make headway into righteousness. The best performance may put you ahead of other people, but you are still being forced downstream. Self-righteousness only seems successful when we are looking at others instead of looking at the current against us. The flesh can never produce righteousness; we can only be slightly less sinful than other people of the flesh.

The law was given to people who were sinful creatures of the flesh with the command, "There is the way of righteousness, give it your best shot." It's the call for people who are weak to battle the current that is mighty. It's a call to do the impossible. Impossible for man, but already accomplished by God.

Grace displaced the law by driving the river back to its beginning with the invitation to walk with Christ. In Him, the river has no power. The invitation is not to fight against the current, but to step into the Spirit where the raging current has been completely done away with.

You are being asked to obey from a position of accomplishment. You are not trying to merit acceptance with God or accomplish righteousness for God. You are already righteous and fully accepted before the command even comes into view. Faith helps us to understand our position in Christ, and that's when the command stops being a merit system in our eyes and becomes a call to trust. You've already tasted the goodness of the Lord, now the commandment is given as a call to stay in the Spirit because of our faith in God's word.

If we believe God is good, we'll trust that God's command is good. If we believe God is depriving us, sin will look tempting.

Sin is not tempting to the satisfied soul, but if we are starving ourselves from fellowship with God, sin looks good. Or as the Bible says, "To the hungry soul, every bitter thing appears sweet."[46]

A Christian that neglects the privilege of walking by faith will constantly battle temptation. To the Christian that is experiencing God, the invitation of temptation appears foolish. A satisfied soul loathes sin, but a starving soul readily consumes it.

This is why God spends so much time trying to convince us of His love and acceptance. Everyone falls into the flesh at various times. The thriving Christian will sin, recognize the flesh for what it is, and will immediately return to walking in the Spirit – which is to walk by faith. They believe God, so when the flesh grips them, they easily break free by trusting in the throne of grace. They don't feel rejected by God, so they don't grovel in the flesh and punish themselves with guilt and shame. Because they are growing in their trust in God's abounding love, this Christian begins outgrowing the flesh, then sin and sinful habits begin falling away.

The one who does not believe in God's unconditional acceptance and rejects the command of God to boldly (or confidently) come to the throne of grace, will walk in defeat. Then when they have done enough self-penance, they may begin to feel accepted again, but when another sin defeats them, then back into the desert of guilt they go. It is not God banishing them from the abundant life; it is disbelief that causes them to abandon His gift of life.

Let me give an illustration. Nearly every illustration breaks down at some point, but we can still use earthly examples to help us understand spiritual truths.

I have two dogs. One loves to curl up next to me and relax or get petted. The other is a passive-aggressive dog. He's not cuddly, but he's also nonaggressive. But he can't stand to see the other dog getting attention. To keep the other dog from getting affection, he'll grab a toy and bring it to the other one and taunt.

---

[46] Proverbs 27:7

Many times it works, and off the cuddling dog will go in pursuit of the toy.

If that doesn't work, my dog will try to provoke the other to wrestle with him. He'll taunt and frolic until the mission is accomplished. He's not really being friendly, but the other dog can't recognize the plot to deprive his rival of affection.

In many ways, Satan does this in the life of the believer. When he sees us growing close to the Lord, he baits us with temptation. If that doesn't work, he'll provoke us. He knows our weaknesses, and will use pleasure or people to draw us back into the flesh. His only goal is to stop you from experiencing the joy of life in the Spirit.

When tempted, those who are weak in faith and still don't believe in the fullness of God's grace, will feel they have betrayed God. And Christians project their feelings of inadequacy onto God. If they feel they have let God down, they assume that God feels betrayed, angry, or disappointed in them. That's how we would feel, so that must be the way God feels toward us. But this is inaccurate.

God is never disappointed, for in order to be disappointed, someone has to have unmet expectations. God sees the end from the beginning, and He knew your failures before you failed. Yet, He loves you anyway. His goal is to rescue you from failure, not hold you accountable for it.

The Bible says, "God is love." This is the nature and essence of God. The word 'love' is the Greek word 'agape'. Here is how the Bible defines agape, **1 Corinthians 13:4-8a**

4 Love suffers long *and* is kind; love does not envy; love does not parade itself, is not puffed up;

5 does not behave rudely, does not seek its own, is not provoked, thinks no evil;

6 does not rejoice in iniquity, but rejoices in the truth;

7 bears all things, believes all things, hopes all things, endures all things.

8 Love never fails.

The first thing to note is that love never fails. This means even if you fail, God's love does not. You are in God's love through Christ, and it transforms you into God's image. This includes your outward behavior, but only as you learn to trust in God's love.

Love is patient and kind. This means when you blow it, love doesn't become unkind, but patiently works to draw you into intimate fellowship, by revealing God's love for you, regardless of whether you feel deserving or not.

Love is not provoked and thinks no evil. This means that once you are in God's love (which you are if you are in Christ), there is nothing you can do to provoke God again. In the Old Testament, in Isaiah 53, God foretells that the coming Messiah (Jesus) would be punished for our sins, bruised for our iniquities, and He would bear the chastisement of the law so we could have peace with God. Then we are promised the New Covenant, where sins are removed and God's favor is a certainty. Then God gives this amazing promise in **Isaiah 54:9**

For this *is* like the waters of Noah to Me; For as I have sworn That the waters of Noah would no longer cover the earth, So have I sworn That I would not be angry with you, nor rebuke you.

The covenant of agape love is as certain as the promise that the world can never again be destroyed by a flood. God has also made a covenant that any who enter Christ by faith, can NEVER be under God's anger again. Nor will God rebuke our sins again, for they have been removed and eradicated in Christ.

This agrees with the New Testament message of love. God cannot be provoked, for wrath has been satisfied in Christ and agape love flows uninhibited. It's not dependent upon you, or your ability to not sin, but is the unchangeable love of God that He has invited you to enter by faith. Sin invites us back into the flesh where pain and sorrow abound. Faith invites us into God's presence, regardless of what happened in the flesh.

In 1 Corinthians 13:5 above, the Bible says, "Love thinks no evil." This is a little unclear in the English. Let's dig out some truth by looking at the original Greek. Love 'logizomai' (reckons, accounts, or credits) no 'kakos' (wrongs, injuries, wickedness).

Or to state it plainly, Love does not account your wrongs. Is this not exactly what God promised in Isaiah 54?

God is love, and love does not credit you with your wrongs. Or as Romans 4:7-8 puts it, "Blessed is the one whose lawless deeds are forgiven and whose sins are covered. Blessed is the one in whom the Lord WILL NOT impute sin."

The commandments and warnings of the New Testament are not intended to defeat you. They are intended to guide you away from the entrapments of the flesh, while leading you to the blessings of the Spirit. They are not intended to create guilt, condemnation, or make you feel unworthy to come before God's throne. You are commanded to be confident in God's presence, but this isn't possible for the one who is comparing themselves against an impossible standard.

Does this mean there are no consequences to sin? No, there are consequences, but defeating the work of Christ is not one of those consequences. Sin is of the flesh and remains in the flesh. Even if you are not actively sinning, your flesh is still in sin. Look at **Romans 7:23**

> But I see another law in my members, warring against the law of my mind, and bringing me into captivity to the law of sin which is in my members.

The Bible goes through great efforts to teach you that sin cannot enter the life of the Spirit, but sin always remains in the flesh. If we live in the flesh, we will experience the sin of the flesh. In the flesh you cannot please God.[47] This is true even if you are trying to serve God. You cannot use your self-efforts to change the nature of the flesh, but you can walk in the Spirit and allow the life of the Spirit to impart life in the flesh. This is explained in **Romans 8:10-11**

> [10] And if Christ *is* in you, the body *is* dead because of sin, but the Spirit *is* life because of righteousness.
> [11] But if the Spirit of Him who raised Jesus from the dead dwells in you, He who raised Christ from the dead will also

---

[47] Romans 8:8

Boundaries Between Faith and Flesh

give life to your mortal bodies through His Spirit who dwells in you.

The same power that raised Jesus from the dead is working to give you life that is unhindered by sin. By faith you receive the power of the Spirit, and then His life breathes life into your mortal bodies. That is the power to overcome sin, and is not dependent upon you 'getting your life right.' This is the power that gets your life right.

Even if you are in Christ, the body is still dead because of sin. Sin still remains in the body. This means if you are trusting in the flesh, sin is always the result. But look at the promise. The power of the Spirit gives life to your flesh. It is not you that brings the flesh under control. It is you who must learn to walk by faith and trust in the promise that the life of the Spirit will overcome sin in your body. This is what brings your outward behavior in line with the inner life you experience when you walk by faith in the Spirit.

This cannot work the other way around. And when the flesh overcomes us, the answer is not to remain in the flesh, groveling in shame and guilt. We are called to look to God's throne of grace with the full assurance that the Spirit will give us the power to live by a standard that is humanly impossible. And it won't be you forcing yourself to do what you don't want to do. It will be a delight to obey, because you will be obeying out of a position of life, instead of out of a position of weakness.

The legalistic mind worries that Christians will get away with sin, not knowing that legalism is just as fleshly as blatant acts of sin. However, the Bible also answers the burning question, what about sin in the Christian's life? As discussed earlier, everything of the flesh is sin, so the goal is not to convert the flesh, but to learn how to invest our lives in the Spirit. This passage helps to explain this. Look at **Galatians 6:7-8**

7 Do not be deceived, God is not mocked; for whatever a man sows, that he will also reap.

8 For he who sows to his flesh will of the flesh reap corruption, but he who sows to the Spirit will of the Spirit reap everlasting life.

Do you see God's anger in this passage? Certainly not. The word 'mock' means to sneer at or thumb the nose at what God has said. All the commandments of God protect and guide, but if we scoff at God's commands and determine our ways are better, there are consequences, and they are not the judgment of God. They are the reaping of sin.

If you plant thorns, can you expect tulips? If you plant poison ivy, can you expect grapes? No, what you plant is what's going to come up. And if we plant an invasive plant, it's hard to eradicate it.

The same is true in your life and mind. What you sow is what you can expect to reap. If you sow murmuring and complaining, will you reap joy? If you sow anger, will you reap peace? If you sow lust, can you expect purity?

This is the message of the boundaries of sin in the Bible. It is not a warning that God will return His anger upon us, withdraw His love, or no longer accept us as His child. It is the warning that if we invest our lives in the flesh, we can expect fleshly things to overrun our minds and lives. It's easy to point at the adulterer as a sinner. In fact, when a nationally syndicated television minister partnered with an author to write against what they call hyper-grace, their examples were adulterers, people in homosexuality, and other people who lived for the flesh as examples of the dangers of not being afraid of judgment. This is what they claimed would be the fruit of grace believing. Of course, they acknowledged that most examples of moral failure in the church were not grace teachers, but as one put it, "Hyper-grace can give them an excuse for their sin."

Hopefully at this point you can see the absurdity of this claim, but there is a deeper contradiction the legalist doesn't see. Sexual sin is not the primary sin plaguing the church. Self-righteousness is up there, but that isn't even the biggest threat. The biggest threat is pride. It's the belief that my sins are insignificant. At least I'm not an adulterer, so God has to accept me, right?

Pride says, "I have made myself righteous for God." Pride says, "At least I don't struggle with homosexuality." Pride

Boundaries Between Faith and Flesh

believes that if I can swim fast enough against the current of sin so that I'm ahead of 'those sinners', I must be doing something right. Never mind that the self-righteous heart can't perceive that they are still being swept downstream. For the most accomplished religious person, the end result is the same as it is for those they look down upon. Pride says that trusting Christ isn't enough. Man has to do his part, for the work of the cross can't be sufficient without our help.

What about the person who invests their life in their job? Jesus gave an example of a fool who invested his life in this world, became successful, and put his trust in his own wealth. Jesus did not condemn this man for being wealthy or successful. He said he was a fool because he was laying up treasures for this life, but was not rich toward God.[48]

We are investing in the flesh when we allow TV to crowd out so much of our time that we have nothing left to invest in the Spirit. The same is true for sports, hobbies, relationships, and even ministry.

Those who sow in the Spirit will reap the things that pertain to everlasting life. Sowing in the Spirit does not mean working harder for God. It doesn't even mean reading your Bible more. Investing in the Spirit can be found in **Matthew 6:33**

> But seek first the kingdom of God and His righteousness, and all these things shall be added to you.

This passage does not say to work for God, nor does it say to build God's kingdom. It does not tell us to become righteous for God. We are to seek God's kingdom and seek God's righteousness, both of which are already established by God and given to all who seek it. Take time to meditate upon and commit to memory this foundational passage on seeking – **Hebrews 11:6**

> But without faith *it is* impossible to please *Him*, for he who comes to God must believe that He is, and *that* He is a rewarder of those who diligently seek Him.

---

[48] Luke 12;21

Where is work? What are we building, doing, or accomplishing to make God accept us? What great ministry must we do to earn God's reward? Where is sin mentioned in this passage?

Unless your life is built upon faith in what God has done, so that you believe enough to diligently seek God, you will never please God. You can swear off tobacco, liquor, women, and romance novels, but none of that will make you pleasing to God. If you lock yourself in a room where it is impossible to sin, you still cannot please God.

God is pleased with those who walk by faith – focused on the glory of God's grace given through Christ, and He rewards those who seek His fellowship of agape love. If you do these things, sin will fade into the background. If you neglect these things, sin will never lose its stronghold. Sin may disguise itself in ways that appear acceptable to you, but it doesn't change that the body is dead because of sin; therefore, any who live according to the flesh cannot please God. regardless of what they do or don't do.

If you invest your life in faith, you will reap the things of the Spirit, and this will overflow into your life of the flesh. If you invest your life in the flesh, you will never experience the fruit of the Spirit.

The real answer is to stop focusing on sin and start focusing on faith. Trust in God's promise that He will subdue your iniquities. Trust in the promise that God's Spirit will give life to your mortal body. Sin is only subdued by the Spirit. To help understand this, look at **Romans 8:13**

> For if you live according to the flesh you will die; but if by the Spirit you put to death the deeds of the body, you will live.

Of course this was written to those who were trusting in the law for salvation, which applies to the flesh, but the principle of life applies to the Christian. Only the Spirit can put to death the deeds of our sinful flesh. If you trust in the Spirit, you will find life. If you live according to the flesh, you will reap the death of the flesh. Let me reiterate, this is not only blatant sins, but also

Boundaries Between Faith and Flesh

trying to obey God by human effort. The flesh cannot please God – even at its best. Sin cannot defeat the work of Christ – even at its worst.

My prayer is that our exploration of the scriptures teaching on sin has helped you understand that God has given you everything you need to have confidence and assurance in this Christian life. God has proven that sin has no power, and sin is no longer your concern. It's His concern. Your concern is to trust in His grace and stop empowering sin. Stop giving sin undo homage. It has no power. Satan was defeated at the cross. All he can do is deceive you into believing in sin, disbelieving in God's promise, devaluing the work of Christ, and distracting you from walking by faith. Let's end this chapter with **Jude 1:20-21**

> 20 But you, beloved, building yourselves up on your most holy faith, praying in the Holy Spirit,
> 21 keep yourselves in the love of God, looking for the mercy of our Lord Jesus Christ unto eternal life.

You do not build your faith, for faith is not a human attribute. It is most holy because it is a gift from the Most Holy God. You are commanded to build your life upon the most holy faith you have been given through the Spirit. And how to you build your life upon faith? By keeping yourself in the love of God as you trust in His mercy. Mercy is God's promise not to give you the punishment you deserve. Or as we saw earlier, God blessed you with the promise that He will not impute your sin to you.

Through prayer, you are establishing yourself in the fellowship of God, trusting in His mercy, and keeping yourself in God's agape love. Will you obey this command? Are you going to trust in your own worthiness? Will you withdraw from God's love when you feel unworthy, or will you believe God's declaration over you? Will you believe in the enemy's proclamation of your condemnation, or God's declaration, "There is therefore now no condemnation to those who are in Christ Jesus?"

The power of sin has been broken and you are free to walk uninhibited in fellowship with God. God has given the promise that He has taken on the responsibility of suppressing sin and bringing the body of sin under subjection, so you could be free to walk by faith, focusing on Christ and not your struggles.

It's time to leave sin in the grave and reach toward the high calling of God. Trust the word and walk by faith! Never forget God's warning that no flesh will have glory in His presence. Not one person will stand before God and be declared worthy because of what they have done for God. The gospel is not about what you do for God; it's about what God has done for you. It is as **Ephesians 1:6** states, all is:

> To the praise of the glory of His grace, by which He has made us accepted in the Beloved.

The Christian life is about you understanding that everything is about grace. God has made you completely accepted in Christ, so you can understand the glory of His grace. Once you recognize the power of God's love for you, praise of His grace will be the overflow of your heart. You are beloved because you are in the Beloved – Jesus Christ. Faith in His grace is the gospel! All others are worthless counterfeits.

Discussion Questions

What does the Bible mean, "Your life is hidden with Christ in God?"

Can sin destroy your life in the Spirit?

What affect does sin have on us?

How does the empty soul view temptation? How does the fulfilled Christian view temptation?

Review 1 Corinthians 13:4-8 and 1 John 4:16. What do these tell us about God?

What must you and I do in order to gain God's love?

What can we do to lose God's love?

After Jesus removed sin, why did God swear an oath that He will never again be angry or rebuke us?

Does love credit you with your wrongs? Explain your answer.

Can any act of the flesh be righteous for God?

Can any act of sin defeat the work of God in your life?

Review Romans 8:10-11. How does this apply to your daily life?

Explain what the Bible means, "You will reap what you sow."

Has this book challenged the way you view the Christian life? Explain why or why not.

Do you feel like your faith is stronger with a deeper look at grace?

Other Recent Books by Eddie Snipes

Watch for upcoming books in the *Founded Upon Grace* series. You may also be interested in these other books by Eddie Snipes. Please take a moment to rate this book on Amazon.

It is Finished! **Step out of condemnation and into the completed work of Christ.**

The Promise of a Sound Mind : God's plan for emotional and mental health

Abounding Grace: Dispelling Myths and Clarifying the Biblical Message of God's Overflowing Grace

Living in the Spirit: God's Plan for you to Thrive in the Abundant Life

Made in United States
North Haven, CT
07 November 2024

59985729R00075